FUNNY SIDE UP

FUNNY SIDE UP

Written and Illustrated
by Guernsey Le Pelley

Compiled and Edited
by Janet Bassemir

Books from

THE CHRISTIAN SCIENCE MONITOR.

Boston, Massachusetts

This book was designed by Yellow Inc., Needham, Massachusetts.

It was typeset in Futura Extra Black Condensed and Garamond Light Condensed by dnh typesetting, inc., Cambridge, Massachusetts.

It was printed and bound in the U.S.A. by Bawden Printing, Inc., Eldridge, Iowa.

The articles in this book originally ran in *The Christian Science Monitor*.

ISBN 0-87510-201-8

CONTENTS

7 . . . . INTRODUCTION

9 . . . . ON TRENDS

19 . . . . CELEBRATING HOLIDAZE

29 . . . . BREAKING RECORDS

35 . . . . FINE STATE WE'RE IN

51 . . . . AT LEISURE

59 . . . . BIG BUCKS

69 . . . . CHOWING DOWN

77 . . . . DOWN TO EARTH

85 . . . . NOTES ON NOISE

91 . . . . OUT OF THE DEEP

97 . . . . ON OTHER THINGS

111 . . . . APPENDIX

An Introduction
or Nightshirts and Pajamas

Many of the fans of "Lightly Le Pelley" may be wondering exactly how the column came about. After approximately twenty happy, productive years cartooning for *The Christian Science Monitor* I retired. However I felt I couldn't completely sever a relationship which had been such an important part of my life. I could not continue cartooning, obviously, but one day sitting on a bench at the local bus stop, I overheard two old gentlemen seriously discussing the pros and cons of wearing nightshirts as opposed to pajamas. (This conversation eventually led me to write one of many "Lightly" essays, and it can be found in this book, entitled, "Pajama talk—on the park bench".) This incident brought back an awareness that there is a lot of amusing nonsense going on in the world, posing as serious thought. Besides, any man who sleeps in a nightshirt deserves to be caught in a hotel evacuation.

Although this story did not turn out to be the original Lightly column, it started me off. Other incidents and opinions down at the town tennis courts crowded it out for first place. Since 1981 approximately 200 "Lightly Le Pelley" articles have appeared in the pages of the *Monitor*, with no end in sight. In the spring of '89 I received a call from Boston, asking me if I would agree to putting some of the "Lightly" essays into a book.

Knowing my shiftless and helter-skelter working habits, it might have taken me years to put it all together, if it hadn't been for the inspired help of Janet Bassemir, who through her talents of selection and persuasive daily phone calls kept everything going forward whenever I started going sideways. I am grateful for her generous contribution of sorting, arranging and compiling a maze of material and keeping order whenever chaos threatened. Which was whenever I saw a deadline and a lot of work staring me in the face.

My grateful thanks, Janet.

—*Guernsey Le Pelley*

ON TRENDS

10 . . . . SHOELESS GUERNSEY

11 . . . . WHAT'S IN A COLOR?

12 . . . . GORGEOUS EXPLOITATION?

13 . . . . CATALOG WORLD

15 . . . . WITH KETCHUP

16 . . . . PAJAMA TALK—ON THE PARK BENCH

17 . . . . BOOK OF THE MONTH

SHOELESS GUERNSEY

Readers, I hope, will forgive me for writing with my shoes off, but lately I'm finding it more and more difficult to think with my shoes on. It isn't a particular type of shoe my feet object to, it's just any shoe at all.

I don't recall exactly when this shoeless condition crept up on me. During the years I was drawing cartoons for the Monitor I always had shoes on in the office. I always wear shoes when I go to the bank or to church. It's when I get in the house that something happens to me, feetwise.

The relationship between shoes and thinking may not be logical. The fact that a person doesn't think with his feet has been pointed out to me by people who study such things, but I know that a person does think better if his feet are comfortable. And cool. And with wall-to-wall carpet under them.

Once when we were entertaining some visitors from out of town my wife looked at me in sudden alarm.

"You haven't any shoes on!" she gasped.

The out-of-towners didn't seem too upset. I think they simply figured it was one of the whimsical things that happens to people when they move to Florida, like riding a tricycle or wearing loud shorts. Or buying bumper stickers that say, "We are spending our children's inheritance."

But Florida is not to blame. I've been gathering information about this shoeless trend and find it's not peculiar to Florida at all but is growing in other parts of the United States, and maybe even Europe.

Perhaps other people have noticed this. It has been going on in such unlikely states as Minnesota and Delaware, where one might suspect that a shoeless person would not be eligible to vote.

If there are complaints, and it becomes necessary for me to put on shoes while writing, I will oblige. But with shoes on, I can't guarantee the quality of my writing.

WHAT'S IN A COLOR?

Bubble gum pink is the new color-of-the-year.

This is the most radical color news since they stopped painting automobiles black. The first person to paint an automobile pink now ranks in importance with the first person to eat an oyster.

Plain pink is bad enough. But "bubble gum" pink suggests something to be eschewed.

But it is definitely the new color. According to tests made at San Bernardino County Correction Department and elsewhere, BGP (we hate to keep saying those words) has a moderating and soothing effect on people, especially children. Persons who tend to be violent become calm and relaxed in rooms painted bubble gum pink. Chewing pink bubble gum, however, does not necessarily produce the same effect.

Allegedly, other colors have different effects. Not everyone agrees with the test results. Some color experts (the color of the experts is not indicated) believe the outcome is never a simple case of black and white.

But there are certain guidelines. Evidently the reason a lot of

> ## PERSONS WHO TEND TO BE VIOLENT BECOME CALM AND RELAXED IN ROOMS PAINTED BUBBLE GUM PINK

restaurants are painted deep red is that the color increases the appetite. People in red restaurants eat more. Not only more, but faster. This makes things easier for the restaurant but not necessarily for the customer.

Because of the association with gum, one might think that a restaurant done in bubble gum pink would cause people to masticate voraciously, but apparently this is not the case. Or else it results in a lot of chewing but not much swallowing.

Colors have also been tried on schoolroom walls. According to some authorities, all the rowdy children can be found in rooms of orange and white. On the other hand, rooms painted in different shades of blue, with floor coverings of soft gray, result in well-behaved children. This seems like a nice thing to know.

But then, why go to all the trouble and expense of painting schools, where children spend only part of their time? Why not paint the children? Children associating with other blue children in gray jackets might be well mannered even outside of school. It ought to be worth trying. At least up to the age of eight.

GORGEOUS EXPLOITATION?

Everybody writes about the exploitation of women, but nobody sues any fashion designers.

Considering the trend against sex discrimination, one would expect a lot of women to get together in a class-action suit and make a case that designers are creating styles for them to wear that don't do them justice.

Or is it just that deep down women feel that without the tiniest bit of exploitation along feminine lines things would get awfully dull?

According to our private surveys, some small progress against discrimination is being made. For the past millennium, no fat female could get a job as a fashion model. All the new styles would be shown to the public on skinny models, then they would be made into clothes in Sri Lanka, so, as an end result, they would fit anybody.

> **WORST OF ALL, EVERYTHING HAS PLEATS. IF A FELLOW HUGS A WOMAN THESE DAYS HE GETS A CHORD IN G-MINOR.**

Things seem to be changing. One hopes for the better.

When one encounters these new fashions moving through a hotel lobby it is hard to believe there is a woman inside them. One can only hope they are not the same shape as the clothes.

One year's fashions featured huge, ungraceful, floppy pants which must have been a reverse exploitation from "Gentlemen Prefer Hanes." They were so large an average woman had to take three steps before they moved.

And the jackets! They either have football shoulder pads inside or women have been overexploited with aerobics.

But worst of all, everything has pleats. Big, accordion-style pleats. If a fellow hugs a woman these days he gets a chord in G minor.

Or, as that sly woman exploiter, Henny Youngman, says, "Take my wife, pleats!"

CATALOG WORLD

No one can fully realize the dizzy heights to which American civilization has risen until he reads the Hammacher Schlemmer catalog.

For instance, there seems to be a modern demand for a solar-powered ventilated pith helmet. This helmet has a built-in solar-powered fan that blows on one's sweltering head as he walks through the jungle—or up Fifth Avenue, as the case may be. It is not something one would want to be without if his friend had one.

There is also an electric ice cream scoop, and it is strange the need for this has not emerged until now. By plugging it into a wall socket it digs out hard-frozen ice cream in neat, perfectly formed scoops and thus is an aid to the tired housewife, or whatever happens to be in the kitchen these days, including robots.

Then I must mention the Oshibori Towel Hot Basket, which enables anyone to furnish hot towels to guests at the dinner table. The occasion for needing hot towels at the dinner table can be a challenging innovation for any hostess. But if she is totally devoid of originality it can still be transformed into a receptacle for hot rolls.

Golfers in retirement communities should like the 17-in-one golf club. This makes it possible to carry only one club around a golf course, thus eliminating the need of bag or cart. When one is ready to hit the ball, he just adjusts a dial for whatever kind of shot.

Many people would like the talking bathroom scale with a built-in memory. In a clear, digitally synthesized voice, this item announces your weight and tells you how much you have gained or lost since the last time. When you get off, it says, "Have a good day."

And, it might be pointed out, it says, "Have a good day" no matter what nasty things you may have said to it previously.

It is indeed a new world, in which we are all being prepared to love our fellow gadgets.

WITH KETCHUP

No American gastronome worthy of the name can be unaware of the important epicurean contest currently going on among McDonald's, Burger King, and Wendy's.

Which of these modern, gourmet establishments represents the best American cuisine? Who can decide it? It may have to be decided by a panel of chefs from the French Cordon Bleu, because average Americans can no longer recognize food at all, unless it is deep-fried and placed in some sort of paper receptacle.

Even when food can be recognized by sight, many diners cannot recognize it by taste. Products of similar texture, such as fish fillet, chicken, French fries, or hamburger, are not really considered edible until covered with ketchup, or some kind of brown or red sauce, which gives everything a basic, mildly spicy "food taste," widely accepted as "flavor."

McDonald's gives the impression it sells the largest quantity. Outside each McDonald's a huge red sign indicates that over 40 billion have been sold, without specifically designating what. The product sold inside, or through a window, is referred to as a "Mac" or even a "Big Mac." Such items are served in folded cardboard containers, and the wonders therein are not disclosed until one gets to his seat and opens them.

Allegations that a number of people have inadvertently eaten the box covered with ketchup with the sandwich still inside have not been verified to our satisfaction. There have been no complaints of this nature, so if it has ever happened the consumer was not aware of his mistake.

Burger King suggests that although they may be slightly behind in the quantity sold, they are out ahead in the quality. Parking lot connoisseurs, in Burger King territory, claim that because the meat is cooked over an open flame, rather than fried, it is tastier. Basic ketchup taste notwithstanding.

Wendy's, coming on strong, seems to be a cheerful challenger. It is the one, they have decided, who serves the great, original, old-fashioned, real American hamburger. At least, they tend to call it a hamburger and claim it is more juicy.

Meanwhile chefs at the Ritz, Antoine's, etc., watch all this in horror as a creeping number of their refined patrons ask for ketchup.

PAJAMA TALK—ON THE PARK BENCH

There is a bench in the middle of town where lots of conversation goes on while people sit waiting for the bus. Two executive-type codgers sharing a newspaper were sitting there recently, probably retired from a large banking firm, so I moved closer hoping to hear some useful information.

"Nightshirts are coming back," said the one with crisp mustache and horn-rimmed glasses, obviously a bank president.

"I didn't know they'd been away," said his partner, more the vice-president type.

"Are you kidding? When have you seen anyone around in a nightshirt lately?" said Bank President.

"Where would I go," asked VP, "to see people in nightshirts?"

"I mean on television. In a bedroom scene on television have you seen any nightshirts?"

"I haven't seen any pajamas, either. Or even nightgowns!"

Bank President tapped his part of the paper. "Seriously. It says right here you'll be seeing more nightshirts from now on. They're gaining in popularity. I'm thinking of getting a couple."

VP shook his head. "Pajamas are more popular, I don't care what the paper says. What do they know? I'll bet pajamas sell 10 to 1 over nightshirts."

"Harry, they take surveys on these things. Nightshirts are more popular abroad, places like England, Germany, Russia . . ."

"Russia?" Harry blurted. "Who knows how they sleep in Russia? Who sees a Russian in a nightshirt?"

"We're talking about news items. They have *glasnost* in Russia. It means more openness. That goes with nightshirts. Besides, they have nightshirts in red, you know."

"Well," said Harry. "Pajamas seem more normal and respectable, somehow. Even for a Russian . . ."

"Pajamas are a nuisance. You always have to button the dumb things and tie up the pants. Why make sleeping so complicated?"

Harry shook his head. "You don't have to wear the bottoms. You could just wear the tops."

Bank President gloated. "Then that's practically a nightshirt!"

The bus came. The two climbed aboard, leaving me with an idea of what retired bankers talked about.

The woman sitting next to me on the bench leaned my way. "You know, I've heard Burt Reynolds wears a nightshirt."

I looked at her without comment. I'm a pajama man myself.

BOOK OF THE MONTH

Fidel Castro, according to certain unnamed sources, is going to write a book.

Actually, it is alleged he is going to write three books. The first one is to be about the failure of religion. The second one is to be about the failure of economics. The subject of the third seems to be still undecided, but this is not considered a serious omission since he has a wide selection of failures to choose from.

Having Fidel Castro write about the failure of religion seems a bit like having him write about the failure of electric shavers. And, the same might be said about economics. The biggest problem Castro has in economics is getting bills mailed off to Moscow at the end of the month.

Also, he can keep on selling sugar to the Russians, which simplifies his farm program because Cubans try to avoid planting any other crop.

Speculation has started among Castro-watchers as to what particular failure his third book will be about. It is almost certain not to be about his failure to become leader of the third world. He may secretly gloat that Miami has achieved the highest crime rate in the United States, but there again, it is unlikely he would write a whole book about it.

But there must be something Fidel knows less about than religion and economics.

Barbershops? No, it would have to be something more closely related to the capitalistic world.

Maybe something along the lines of disproving that old capitalistic adage, "Clothes make the man." It can be reliably said Fidel Castro is not a clotheshorse.

Of course, he may think he has resisted capitalistic fashion trends by wearing the same uniform he had when he first came to Cuba, but he is mistaken. In American TV video and rock concert crowds he would be considered well dressed. Come to think of it, if Castro could play a few chords on a guitar and walk out on a stage with Madonna, he would be a smash.

It might get his third book out of the failure rut.

CELEBRATING HOLIDAZE

20 . . . . HAPPY NEW YEAR!

21 . . . . JUST SAY NOEL

22 . . . . BOUQUETS FOR FATHERS

23 . . . . TRIVIA DAY

25 . . . . CHARMING WEEK

26 . . . . A DAY OF THANKS AND GIVING

27 . . . . CHRISTMAS SHOPPING

HAPPY NEW YEAR!

New Year's Day is a federal holiday on which people make New Year's resolutions. By so doing they raise a benign hope they won't repeat last year's mistakes. Mostly the mistakes are repeated, but as they say, it's the thought that counts.

By and large, holidays are a good thing, even though they lack consistency and lose some of their original purpose. Technically the United States doesn't have "national" holidays, except in the District of Columbia, since the making and observance of holidays is reserved to the states. Generally the states don't complain much and let Washington go ahead, except in a few cases when states think they are getting pushed around.

New Year's Day, being nonreligious and nonpolitical, doesn't bother anyone. People are just glad to have a day to sleep off New Year's Eve. Except for Jews, Chinese, Muslims, and many others, it officially starts a new year. *Whose* new year doesn't seem to matter as long as everyone gets the day off. Labor Day also fits into the category of wholehearted acceptance. It is primarily to ensure a day of rest for the "worker," but all the bosses take it off

as well, just to show no discrimination.

Then there is Columbus Day, which slightly annoys those strict and literal history buffs. They readily agree that Columbus discovered Watlings Island, or whatever, but it was that Italian, sailing for England, John Cabot, who actually found the American mainland first. The indomitable Norsemen notwithstanding, Columbus was probably the greatest navigator the world has known, so we might as well keep the holiday.

Many states assert their own holidays. Missouri has its Harry S. Truman Day, Alabama celebrates Thomas Jefferson, but as far as I know, North Carolina doesn't have a day for James Polk. New York doesn't take notice of Martin Van Buren, either, but there is a sort of celebration on Verrazano Day, April 7. Giovanni da Verrazano discovered that big bridge across the narrows of Lower Bay going to Staten Island.

The solution for national holidays might be for them to come at certain, regularly appointed intervals and simply be called "Days Off." Except for New Year's Day. It's nice to say "Happy New Year."

JUST SAY NOEL

Christmas is upon us. We made it one more time.

Each year my wife and I timidly approach the season by saying, "Now, we're not going to make a lot of Christmas this year. Don't buy me anything." Perhaps other people say this, too. We say it, I think, in fear of falling short of what is expected of us.

Christmas just seems too big a thing to encounter every year. One can enter upon other holidays like Washington's Birthday, the Fourth of July, or Arbor Day without obligation. They are simply *there*. One has a picnic, or whatever, and that is that.

But Christmas enters our consciousness bigger than life, demanding—in the spirit of love and goodwill—that we shape up spiritual-wise. My wife thinks the spirit of Christmas is so pervasive that it touches even the birds around our house. Cranky, the snowy egret, and Fishface, the great white heron, get treats of smelts, on the assumption that they, too, can feel the brighter promise in the world. Rollo, the pelican, does a clumsy dance of joy over a tidbit.

Christmas consumes thought. The record-breaking crowds that flock to stores the day after Thanksgiving establish for the press and public a barometer as to the success or failure of Christmas. Somehow the world seems betrayed if sales are down, as if people of goodwill don't realize their debt to their fellowman.

Despite all our evasions and protestations, Christmas comes on relentlessly. The little red-ribboned gifts—like pledges to do better—appear as usual on Christmas morn. A rather unpretentious Christmas tree returns with well-used decorations from last year, and the year before, and the year before that. On top is the slightly crooked silver star from ages past, shining rather faintly through its tarnish.

Christmas is here once more. We feel good in spite of ourselves. And the light of the star, after all, is really in our hearts.

BOUQUETS FOR FATHERS

Father's Day is not, as one might suppose, a male version of Mother's Day.

In the first place a man didn't even think it up. A woman did. Mrs. John Bruce Dodd, in 1909, persuaded the Ministerial Society of Spokane, Wash., to have a church service devoted to the fathers of the community—presumably to pray for them. They may have been off playing golf instead of coming to church.

Although Spokane started praying for fathers in 1909, it was not until 1924 that President Calvin Coolidge, hardly a great father-image, recommended the day for national observance.

Mother's Day was promoted for the honor and respect—if not the reverence—of motherhood. But Father's Day? The reason for Father's Day, according to official words from the White House, was, in part, "To impress upon fathers the full measure of their obligations." That hardly sounds like a hymn of jubilant praise. It somehow conjures up a picture of fathers sneaking out the back door when the rent is due and the baby is crying.

Mother's Day has become international. For whatever

> **GENERALLY ONE DOESN'T TAKE DAD OUT TO DINNER. IT'S BETTER TO LET HIM BURN A STEAK ON THE GRILL IN THE BACKYARD.**

reason, the world's homage towards mother has made the day a smashing commercial success, compared with a somewhat impecunious Father's Day. Greeting card business aside, in the two weeks before Mother's Day flower shops do a landslide business, phone lines bog down, candy sales skyrocket, restaurants serve long lines. The variety of gifts appropriate for mom adds significantly to the country's gross national product growth and gives Christmas a run for the money.

Yet fathers seldom know when Father's Day is and would feel embarrassed if too much were made of it. Generally one doesn't take dad out to dinner. It's better to let him burn a steak on the grill in the backyard. Although the red or white rose is said to be the Father's Day symbol, he would feel foolish getting a bouquet. In short, fathers are very happy with the status quo.

Down at the town tennis courts, one chap said his daughter gave him a box of chocolates but there were four pieces missing. He thinks they were the maple creams.

TRIVIA DAY

There may be those who don't take notice of such a trivial event, but Jan. 3 was Trivia Day.

Trivia has become important in the past two decades, and just because certain information is useless doesn't mean it isn't an essential part of everyone's life. Come to think of it, how much important information do we know? Not much. We get most of it from television, a source of great dubiosity.

Knowing the fact that Florida has the lowest high point in the United States won't buy any groceries, but someone has to know it. Joseph Palmer's name won't be found in a list of great American statesmen, but he was the first American man (outside of certain religious groups) to wear a beard in public. If anyone has taken the trouble to notice, all the early Founding Fathers were clean shaven. Mr. Palmer was even put in jail because of his whiskers.

It is a matter of triviality, perhaps, that today American men spend 154,000 minutes in a lifetime shaving.

She doesn't appear on any of the music charts, but Effie Crocker wrote "Rock-a-Bye-Baby." Probably no one ever thought of "Rock-a-Bye-Baby" as ever being written at all, but there you are. Somebody had to do it. The words are from Mother Goose.

One thing I have not been able to trace. What is the dividing line between trivia and important information? The price of a yak is certainly trivia, unless you happen to live in Tibet and need to buy one.

No one thinks it important to know that a snail can move at a speed of 0.03 m.p.h. It may have some relative importance to a snail, however, if he is planning a trip. It could be of use to know that an elephant can run 25 m.p.h. In case one ever gets chased by an elephant, he can figure his chances of escape on a sort of 50-50 basis.

Trivia Day passed without much notice—which is perhaps the way it should be. How much can one celebrate something without spoiling its triviality? It may be an item of trivia to know how many people knew it was Trivia Day.

If it was more than 1 in 1,000, it might kick it out of the ranks of trivia and into the importance of National Maritime Day.

CHARMING WEEK

This summer had more than its share of tension, toughness, and tumult. There were, among other situations, the peppery and preachy Iran-contra hearings; the ever-explosive situation in the Gulf; the massacres in India's Sikh-Hindu conflict; and street fighting in the Philippines and South Korea.

Many may not have known that at one point during this time we were also going through Snow White Week.

Snow White Week! If it did nothing else it reminded us that once we lived in a different world.

In case there are some moderns who never heard of Snow White, she was a princess whose beauty was envied by a wicked witch. In fear of her life S.W. fled to the forest, where she was taken care of by seven dwarfs. But alas, the wicked witch finally got the upper hand and S.W. ate a poisoned apple and was given up for dead. Then along came a genuine Prince on a real white horse, who kissed her and she revived. Where can one find kisses

> ## SAY THE WORD "PRINCE" TODAY AND ONE CONJURES UP A CONTROVERSIAL FIGURE, GYRATING IN A ROCK VIDEO

like that now? It was love at first sight and they rode off into the sunset.

Once upon a time every kid in town knew the names of the seven dwarfs, but I wasn't sure if today they even knew Snow White. I took an unofficial poll down at the beach and was surprised to find that Snow White still has a big following. A few answers fell by the wayside. One little girl thought her sister had the Snow Whites' new record album, and one other thought it had something to do with the war on drugs. But it wasn't a bad result, considering.

Say the word "Prince" today and one conjures up a controversial figure, gyrating in a rock video, whose kiss, many believe, is more akin to the poison apple than the restorative and therapeutic osculations of HRH Charming. Still, HRH Charming and his trusty steed have been going onward for 50 years and are evidently still in the secret hearts of young damsels.

That in itself is a kind of solid gold record.

A DAY OF THANKS AND GIVING

Thanksgiving should be of the heart and not of the stomach. People should remember that eating is not a form of prayer.

There are many countries which set aside a time to offer thanks, but the American Thanksgiving Day is probably the one most vigorously pursued. Basically it commemorates the celebration of the Pilgrims in the Plymouth colony in 1621 for the abundant and life-saving harvest, the importance of which perhaps cannot be fully felt in today's affluent society.

In fact today, where there is so much surrounding us to be grateful for, we may tend to become inured and be grateful for nothing.

The original Thanksgiving feast lasted three days and included the neighboring Indians, who contributed much in the way of knowledge of how to survive in an untamed land. But the point of the holiday is lost if we forget that the feast is only a symbol. The well-stocked Thanksgiving table at Plymouth was

THE WELL-STOCKED THANKSGIVING TABLE AT PLYMOUTH WAS THE PHYSICAL EVIDENCE OF A HEAVENLY BLESSING.

the physical evidence of a heavenly blessing. It demonstrated the promise that it would be possible to live through another winter. The Pilgrims were well aware of the benevolent hand of Providence touching their resolute efforts.

When thanks are offered at the beginning of a meal, let's be sure it's not a mumbled ritual—a sort of thanks for the mashed potatoes and gravy and let's get on with it.

If our Thanksgiving is to be a real commemoration of that original celebration in 1621, we will have to be more fully aware of what the event meant to that isolated little band. We should be more aware of the fullness of the blessing that shines on us.

From beginning to end, the life of a Pilgrim was one of giving of themselves, living the faith they had in their God. Each must have understood that his reward came not in more human possessions but in what was gained in quality of spirit.

Shouldn't one's reward for giving come just in the act itself?

CHRISTMAS SHOPPING

I WOULD LIKE TO DISCUSS THE MEANING OF CHRISTMAS....

There have been articles written about organizations that help overcome the drinking habit. I am hoping someone will start a Christmas Shoppers Anonymous.

Most of the year I lead a normal, adjusted life. I can walk past store windows displaying sweaters, ties, or tea sets without seasonal symptoms seizing me by the throat. But a time comes in December, which Christmas itself has nothing to do with, when a feeling of frenzy sets in.

All this may have something to do with too many Santas walking around ringing bells, or it may be too many sound systems playing "Frosty, the Snowman," a jingling tune that works on raw nerves.

Whatever the cause, during these weeks I am sucked into a maelstrom of people who have the same inebriation, rushing from counter to counter with credit cards in their hands.

Perhaps the most disturbing moments come when I get drawn by the current into the "toy" section. If the United States is losing the arms race with the Soviet Union, all Washington has to do is turn the toy manufacturers loose on the problem. If US submarines are equipped with even half of this gadgetry, they are ahead for at least 10 years.

Even the electronic games have an element of Frankenstein creativity that's no less than amazing. And the dolls! The dolls have become smarter than the parents who buy them. I can recall the pleasant wonderment of a child tipping a doll slightly and having it say "mama." Now one picks up a doll and it discusses health measures, birth control, and social problems.

Of course, there is one reassuring aspect to all this. When the actual day of Christmas arrives, the terrible symptoms that seemed to have taken over are dispelled like a mist. All the bells and carols suddenly symbolize a peace that had been there all the time.

But something should be done about that frenzied interval beforehand. If no one comes up with a Christmas Shoppers Anonymous, we will have to think of another answer.

BREAKING RECORDS

30 . . . . CHANDELIER MUNCHING

31 . . . . A RECORD HOLDER

32 . . . . CRACKED RECORDS

33 . . . . IT'S HUGE; IT'S GASTRONOMIC

CHANDELIER MUNCHING

NOW TRY IT WITH SOY SAUCE

One of the books I browse through from time to time is the Guinness Book of World Records. It was started more than 30 years ago by Sir Hugh Beaver, an official of the Guinness Brewing Company, because he was involved in an argument about how fast a golden plover could fly.

I suppose that could be important to some people. Plover chasers, for instance.

As research books go, I would hazard a guess that the Guinness Book of World Records includes more useless information than any other book in the world. It has a bewildering array of facts one could never find anywhere else, including facts found in the Encyclopaedia Britannica.

For example, until I read it in the Guinness Book of World Records, I never knew that someone had eaten a tree. But someone did.

The biggest tree that anyone has ever eaten is an 11-foot birch. I have never eaten a tree myself, so I never imagined anyone else did. It never crossed my mind.

Neither had eating a supermarket cart.

But a Frenchman, Michael Lotito, not only ate a supermarket cart, he ate seven chandeliers, seven television sets, and a Cessna airplane. He also ate a coffin without any ill effects. He may have considered this dessert, since it was mostly wood.

According to those who observed this omnivore, he can consume about two pounds of metal per day. This means, I suppose, that he can't just down a supermarket cart during his lunch hour, but has to dawdle over it like a kid with spinach.

I bring this up because we frequently read in newspapers about what we should and shouldn't eat. Food specialists tell us that practically every fast diet food today is potentially dangerous to our health.

And many people eating at restaurants are scared to death of the tantalizing smell of fried onions wafting from the kitchen.

They have received warnings against eating meats, salty foods, French fries, butter, mayonnaise, gravy, and a lot of other stuff they see on the menu.

Nothing has been said, however, against eating television sets or chandeliers. Or small airplanes.

If people can eat TV sets and stay healthy, a barbecued pork sandwich can't be all bad.

A RECORD HOLDER

Most everyone would like to be remembered for something. Not very many can hope to set a new high-jump record, run a record mile, or land on the moon. This means that a lot of people must strive for less important achievements.

From time to time in the news, some unfulfilled chef cooks up a mile-long sausage to get on TV. Sausages do not gain any more flavor when cooked by the mile, and it certainly doesn't make them any easier to eat. Does one still buy them by the pound or by the tenth of a mile?

People try to get into the Guinness Book of World Records by endlessly jumping rope, or being part of a team that squeezes into a phone booth. An acquaintance of mine even got the idea he could beat the world's record of holding one's breath under water and had to be revived after six unsuccessful attempts.

The most recent effort for fame coming to my attention was a news item about Michael Tora balancing 106 cigar boxes on his chin. Never in my wildest dreams did I imagine this was an event entered in worldwide competition. Evidently it is because Mr. Tora broke the previous world record of 90 cigar boxes, held by someone in Michigan.

THE MOST RECENT EFFORT FOR FAME WAS A NEWS ITEM ABOUT MICHAEL TORA BALANCING 106 CIGAR BOXES ON HIS CHIN.

I remember a high school art teacher who, I am sure, hoped for some wide acclaim for her art. She never achieved recognition. I will never forget her, because she inspired and encouraged me to draw; even to cartoon. She never despaired of my erratic, emerging talent.

Helen Wood is a prime record holder in my heart, and I think she achieved more in her long years of giving of herself to young people trying to find their way than does one balancing 106 cigar boxes on his chin or cooking a mile-long sausage. She didn't get in the Book of Records. It is too bad that achievement is not always obvious.

CRACKED RECORDS

Once in a while I get befogged by what is in the Guinness Book of World Records.

I can understand why a lot of people might find it necessary to learn who is the world's highest pole-vaulter, but the fact that the largest bubble gum bubble blower is also listed disturbs my otherwise rational outlook on life. The record is 19½ inches across, if there is anyone who can't stand not knowing.

There is also the record for shooting someone out of a cannon. It is 175 feet. There is also the odd bit of information along with it—a statistical nuance, no doubt—that a person loses three-eighths of an inch in stature when shot out at a somewhat lesser distance. The competition in the field of being shot out of a cannon is probably small, but it seems a more appropriate record than anything connected with chewing bubble gum.

All this zeal for chronicling takes me back to my college days. Setting some kind of record is evidently part of the human psyche. I recall that my roommate established an impressive record of tossing a quarter into a shoe, on the other side of the room, 77 times without a miss. It was a regulation US quarter and a Size 9½ shoe and a 12½-foot room. This record evidently

I NOTE THAT IN THE BOOK OF RECORDS IT TOOK SOMEONE 15 DAYS TO EAT HIS BICYCLE.

still stands. Another record was set bouncing a tennis ball off a person's head 139 consecutive times, while the target sat on the grass reading Steinbeck.

The record I remember most vividly, however, is the one set eating pancakes in the college dining room on a Sunday morning. It happened around the time of Washington's Birthday, so it possibly had some patriotic significance. Anyway, my classmate ate 38 pancakes with syrup and butter. The runner-up ate 22. I ate only 12. Because there is a pancake-eating record in the Guinness Book of Records of 62 pancakes, it should be pointed out they were all an exact six inches in diameter, whereas the 38 pancakes of college days were considerably larger. Also, real butter and syrup were involved—no present-day culinary substitutes, thank you—if nourishment is any consideration.

Contests that involve eating are hard to regulate with scientific specifications. I note that in the book of records it took someone 15 days to eat his bicycle.

Perhaps something can be said for record bubble gum chewing after all.

IT'S HUGE; IT'S GASTRONOMIC

Recently there was an item coming out of Chicopee, Mass., to the effect that someone there smoked up a kielbasa weighing 412 pounds. It was 26 feet, 3 inches long, too, which must have been a tight fit if it was done in somebody's kitchen. A sausage this size may not set any kind of world record, but I suspect it is the biggest sausage ever to come out of Chicopee.

The question always rises in my mind how anyone eats something like this. Or maybe more to the point, *who* eats something like this? It's not something you just put on a plate. It has to be on something like a flat car. Or at least on a dozen or so kitchen tables.

I suppose consuming a sausage this size isn't as big a problem as I imagine. Probably 300 hungry Polish Chicopeeans could do it. I don't happen to know how many Poles live in Chicopee, but there must be more than a few to think up a stunt like this, and they all must have lively appetites.

It isn't that I am putting down big kielbasa. I like a bit of kielbasa now and then, although it would be an average helping on an average plate. It is great stuff with crisp bread, or even with eggs. But faced with more than 400 pounds of it, I'm not sure I would be able to swallow.

Another thing. Kielbasa is not only famous for its flavor but for its garlic content, and this adds another dimension to this equation.

I have been in a compact car where only three other people had imbibed garlic and I thought I wasn't going to make it to the next spoken sentence.

But 300 people? All carrying on within an invisible vapor of garlic?

However, I am sure this titanic sausage event will have its good results. If I am ever driving through Massachusetts and get the hankering for some kielbasa, I will head for Chicopee just like everyone else who may have read the news item.

By this time, I am sure, kielbasa will be a normal size, on a normal plate, in a normal restaurant, served by a smiling Polish chef who remembers his day of glory.

FINE STATE WE'RE IN

37 . . . . OH, SAY, CAN YOU SING IT?

38 . . . . PITCHING ANTHEMS

39 . . . . IS IDAHO AN INDIAN NAME FOR POTATO?

41 . . . . TUBA CITY

42 . . . . NORTH TO THE WHAT?

43 . . . . COUNTING OTHERS

44 . . . . SPRING CATASTROPHE

45 . . . . THE GETTING OF WISDOM

46 . . . . AMERICA, THE 'HENGED'

47 . . . . APOLOGIES OF THE ABJECT SORT

48 . . . . CHICAGOPHY

49 . . . . D.C. VACATION DAZE

OH, SAY, CAN YOU SING IT?

The tone for future relations between the United States and the Soviet Union will be set for some time to come as a result of the nuclear arms talks which are now under way. The success of our relations with any world nation is determined by the image we have of ourselves. Our main problem is, we haven't grasped our main problem.

We have the wrong National Anthem.

Everyone stands up when the Star Spangled Banner is played, but no one sings it. No one even knows the words. Least of all, those opulent stars of stage and screen who are hired to belt it out at the World Series or Bowl games over amplifiers so everyone else can mouth along with it. We start every ball game with two strikes against us.

To have a National Anthem no one can sing is bad enough, but to have one which keeps on asking offhand questions, such as: "Oh, say, can you see by the dawn's early light . . . ?" and "Oh, say, does that star-spangled banner yet wave . . . ?" isn't even worthy of Victor Herbert. Anyway, we have enough questions already we can't answer.

And, what is this "rockets' red glare, bombs bursting in air" bit? Well, it seems that this is what gives us proof through the night that our flag is still there! Since we never really think about the words, of course we don't consider that if we ever have rockets' red glare from now on, no one in the entire Northern Hemisphere is going to see anything.

We don't mean to imply we can't be proud of the American flag, but do we have to fuzz its identity by calling it a "star-spangled banner"? Good heavens, it sounds like something a chorus girl might wear, jumping out of a cake at the lodge. In short, we are not singing either about our real selves or the real meaning of the flag.

Deep down we know that the best image of ourselves comes through in "America, the Beautiful." We have beautiful, spacious skies; amber waves of grain; majestic purple mountains and plains abundant with fruit which should remind us how bountiful is the grace God sheds upon us. But best of all, our good is crowned with our unique brotherhood from sea to sea. Such a song would help us understand ourselves better.

Once we get our priorities straight, everything else will fall into line.

PITCHING ANTHEMS

Some time ago this column bravely advocated changing the national anthem from "Oh, say can you see . . . ?" to "Oh, beautiful for spacious skies." It brought soap boxes full of letters which were 99 and 44/100ths percent pure. That is, in favor of a change.

Recently, like all good Americans, I watched the World Series. "Oh, say can you see . . . ?" is still being sung incorrectly, if not jived out of recognition. Meanwhile, lines of ballplayers stand chewing gum and blowing the occasional bubble in what appears to be utter boredom while someone besides themselves is giving the pitch.

The "Oh, say" song doesn't have the sanctity of antiquity. It wasn't officially made the national anthem until March of 1931. No one succeeds in singing it as it is written. It may be that everyone thinks his version improves it, or doesn't know the real words and music, or is embarrassed to be singing it in the first place.

After watching the World Series, I decided that if Howard Cosell could be changed for an allegedly better rendition, anything can. The anthem conjures up the ill-advised War of

THE "OH, SAY" SONG DOESN'T HAVE THE SANCTITY OF ANTIQUITY. IT WASN'T OFFICIALLY MADE THE NATIONAL ANTHEM UNTIL MARCH OF 1931.

1812. It is a period piece and doesn't represent the essence of the United States.

The saving grace of "Oh, say" is that its central theme is the flag. But the flag deserves to be seen in better light than the red glare of rockets and the smoke of bursting bombs, which now could be nuclear.

Anthems should express the character of the people who sing them. The US has not only outgrown the War of 1812's youthful stridency but also the one-dimensional patriotism the song advocates.

The 1812-ers may think I'm subversive. While I listen to "Oh, say," I secretly think of spacious skies, fields of grain, majestic purple mountains, and alabaster cities. I even meditate on the good, which Americans—though still imperfectly—have achieved beyond every other country in the world.

And I don't think of the Stars and Stripes as a question mark, about which it must be asked: Oh, say, does it still wave? Its symbol waves in us all, like billowing brotherhood, from sea to shining sea.

IS IDAHO AN INDIAN NAME FOR POTATO?

In the United States, 26 of the states have names of Indian origin. That adds up to a lot of territory and leaves the nation with an indelible memorial to Indian heritage.

I started to think about this when sitting in a restaurant next to a family with a precocious six-year-old who held forth like a 26-year-old going on 40. While playing with the food on his plate, he wanted to know if Idaho was the Indian name for potato. His father didn't think so, not knowing any Irish Indians.

When I got home I went over the names of the states and was surprised to discover that about 26 are related to Indian beginnings.

One might think, with the great westward surge across the continent, that the names of states would tend to commemorate American leaders—people like John Adams, James Madison, and Thomas Jefferson. Or even lesser lights such as Lewis and Clark, Gen. George Custer, or Daniel Boone.

But people must have preferred the sound of Indian names, not only in the West but in the East, where Massachusetts and Connecticut are found.

Of course English names did have some success. Pennsylvania was named for William Penn. But there were also notable failures. An effort was made to name a new state after Benjamin Franklin, and for several years a state was known as Frankland. But the Cherokee villages along the riverbanks known as *tanasi* finally prevailed and the name that endured is Tennessee. It does have a better sound.

Then there is Utah, a name derived from a Navajo word for a Shoshone tribe that lived up on the higher ground. The Mormons, however, wanted to have the state called Deseret, a word in the Book of Mormon that means "Land of the Honeybees." Congress decided against it, so the Indian word, Utah, is still used today.

Somehow there seems to be more music in the Indian words than in the English translation.

When people speak of Iowa, Nebraska, Missouri, and Ohio, they may be aware of the lovely sound of the words without realizing they are continuing to keep alive the way the various Indian tribes described the land: "beautiful land," "broad water," "muddy water," and "good river."

It's time Americans gave credit to the language of the Omahas, Algonquins, and the Iroquois for the better words for naming the states. For instance, there is Michigan. The word is a beautiful Chippewa phrase with a pleasing melody. Much better than "great water."

Now if only all the states could remain as beautiful as the way the Indians saw them.

TUBA CITY

It all started the other day down at the town tennis courts when a fellow got a post card from a town he used to live in called Paradise. His only comment was that if the real Paradise was anything like the town, he would rather go to the other place.

The same fellow complained about a town in Arkansas named Romance. The name seemed to suggest a touch of the adventurous life, but he hadn't been there two hours before a girl slapped his face. Something like that is enough to make a person move to Why, Ariz.

Many towns have simple, honest names, such as Hot Springs and Cold Springs. Do you suppose that at one time all the towns were named Hot Springs because they had some hot springs tucked away in the woods somewhere, but as the hot water ran out, many had to change their name to Cold Springs? Maybe. Maybe not.

I once was in Wawa, Ontario. I remember when I asked a child where I was, I thought I had made her cry.

I never knew anyone, firsthand, who lived in Truth or Consequences, N.M. Superficial research, however, tells me that the inhabitants of Truth or Consequences didn't tell the truth to begin with and so now have to spend the rest of their days in that town suffering the consequences. If I have this wrong, perhaps someone can put me straight.

Tom Bean and Tom Green are two towns in Texas. I presume Tom Bean lives in one and Tom Green in the other. Beyond that I won't venture a comment.

Towns called Moose Jaw or Medicine Hat may have reasonable and valid reasons for acquiring such names, but the name of that town in Wales strikes me as beyond the pale of human tolerance. I, of course, am speaking of Llanfairpwllgwyngyllgogerychwyrndrobwillllantysiliogogogoch. I hope whoever suggested that name has been dealt swift justice.

I find I have more and more respect for people who founded towns and simply named them descriptively, such as South Bend, Twin Forks, Black Lake, Fall River—stuff like that.

Meanwhile, take me back to Bloomer, Wis.

NORTH TO THE WHAT?

Alaska wants to secede from the Union already.

It seems like rather short notice.

At least they talk about it in the wintertime when there is reason to get heated up; and the thing which heats them up most is oil. Not burning it. Talking about it.

Or, to put it more simply, Alaskans don't like some of the policies coming out of Washington.

So, what else is new?

Alaskans get a lot of good points for character. But living as they do with Russians on one side and Canadians on the other, they haven't quite got the idea of who they are, where they are going, or why. It is the only state without a nickname, but it does have a motto, which is: North to the Future. A rather bleak battle cry for anyone living at Point Barrow.

From all reports, Texas is the one state which is delighted at the prospect of Alaska getting out of the Union. Texas never wanted Alaska in the Union to begin with. To a Texan, living in only the second biggest state is like being pulled off his horse by a sheep.

To be absolutely honest, Alaska hasn't been a state long enough to talk about seceding. So far, it has voted Republican only five times. So, as far as any secession talk is concerned, it should get in line and wait its turn. There are a lot of places

> **TO A TEXAN, LIVING IN ONLY THE SECOND BIGGEST STATE IS LIKE BEING PULLED OFF HIS HORSE BY A SHEEP.**

which have put up with Washington's policies a lot longer than Alaska has.

Take Nantucket, Martha's Vineyard, and Cape Cod. They all have had the urge to secede now and then, but they have hung in there and paid their dues, so to speak. Everyone can sympathize. They all have been putting up with national administrations since the capital was New York and everyone can imagine what that was like. Anyway, Nantucketers have some reason for their outcry, with immigrants from other parts of the Union being dumped in there every day by the planeloads. Talk about spoiling the neighborhood!

The big point always seems to be money. Alaskans would like to get richer by selling oil at a high price to Japan instead of at a lower price to the United States. But this windfall would last only 10 years at the most. By that time Japan would be selling the oil back to Alaska at a profit.

Perhaps one problem is that much of the argument comes out of Juneau, the capital, which is barely inside Alaska on the south side. They can get out quicker than anyone else to spend a few winter months in California.

Of course that might not last either. If California gets a few more illegal Mexicans, it will be the next state voting to secede. Come to think of it, that may be Mexico's motto, too: North to the Future.

COUNTING OTHERS

According to someone's unofficial survey, travel agents are reluctant to recommend Miami as a vacation spot these days.

Some statistics show that Miami may have been taken over by wildlife, but it isn't the Everglades. Much of the change is caused by Haitians, illegal Cubans, and other unfeathered people. About 2,000 Indians have moved in from the Everglades. But they are quite peaceful, mostly wrestling alligators and selling wallets and belts for a living.

It is said, somewhat facetiously, that Miami is rapidly gaining the charm of a foreign city. The city has about the same number of Hispanics as it has non-Hispanic whites. The number for each is around 680,000. But Miami is one of the few places where blacks are considered "Anglos" not because blacks are necessarily whiter than Cubans, but because they speak Anglaise

SOME STATISTICS SHOW THAT MIAMI MAY HAVE BEEN TAKEN OVER BY WILDLIFE, BUT IT ISN'T THE EVERGLADES.

rather than Espanol.

The population also contains almost 15,000 Asians. But what adds to the confusion are 70,000 listed as "others."

As yet, we have not interviewed any of the people from Miami known as "others." But since there are so many it is likely one or two will show up at Florida west coast airports reasonably soon. Without the actual designation on the passport, identification may not be easy.

Americans are concerned that the fascination with minorities as separate and distinct, each with its own language and heritage, will cause irreparable damage to America's concept of nationhood.

This new, growing segment of the population known as "others" could be a blessing in disguise.

SPRING CATASTROPHE

Once a year Florida goes through what is called a "Spring Break." Maybe "break" is not the word. Some people call it "Spring Catastrophe."

In case the meaning of the annual phenomenon is obscure to people who live, say, in Akron, Ohio, it is something that happens to college students in the spring, and is manifested by an urge to infest the Florida beaches—like swallows returning to Capistrano. Or perhaps more like vultures swooping in on a garden party. During this time mature Floridians disappear from the beaches, unless they want to walk barefoot over half an acre of unclad stomachs while being thumped on the head with a volley ball. It is said that some students can be around for weeks and never get as far as the water.

This rite seems to be more a boy-girl thing, rather than a need to relax from studying. The pattern is that mostly-naked boys pile into expensive sports cars, while mostly-naked girls get into similar vehicles, then drive around and scream at each other. This is done against the cacophony of cassettes, which on an average day can be heard as far as South Carolina.

The news media apparently believe this is beneficial to the economy. Certainly there is an upsurge in repair bills—entire hotel lobbies have to be replaced and about 30 miles of shoreline has to be restored. Conventional restaurants and the better hotels remain empty during this onslaught, while cheaper sleeping accommodations are anthills of activity.

After about two weeks everything returns to normal. This regenerative process seems to be one of the great restorative facts of nature. It gives hope to all of mother earth.

> **DURING THIS TIME MATURE FLORIDIANS DISAPPEAR, UNLESS THEY WANT TO WALK BAREFOOT OVER HALF AN ACRE OF UNCLAD STOMACHS**

THE GETTING OF WISDOM

There is a nagging impression that ignorance in the United States is spreading faster than Florida state taxes.

According to "60 Minutes," Newsweek magazine, and many other sources, America is failing in standard, basic education. Young people are coming out of high school and college with a level of knowledge far below those in other parts of the industrial world: A package of learning so small it is laughable—or would be, if it weren't so horribly serious.

A column by William F. Buckley Jr. pointed out that Sen. Bill Bradley discovered that 25 percent of college seniors in Dallas couldn't name the country south of the Texas border. One can argue that Texans were always unaware of the microcosm called the rest of the world, but the plague of ignorance is obviously not limited to Texas but is nurtured nationwide. Even in egg-headed Boston, 39 percent of college seniors couldn't name the six New England states.

What is so ominous is that the ignorance is often defended. Why be educated? One can learn a trade, punch a computer, or fix a car without knowing much of anything else. This argument might hold up in the Soviet Union, if it were voiced there— which it isn't—because the Soviet Union is run, for better or worse, by an elite.

But if the US is going to represent democracy in the world successfully, it has to see something as big as the nose on Uncle Sam's face. A democracy is a government by and for the *people*. It is all very well to point out the rightness of this idea, but democracy can succeed in the way it was intended only in a nation of educated, intelligent people. There is nothing achieved in the rule of the uninformed.

Americans are taxed to provide for children's education. Instead of the children's getting educated, many succeed only in getting pregnant. Perhaps one day the public will find grounds for asserting that ignorance itself is immoral, if not sinful.

And as for moral advancement, the Bible provides some advice. Proverbs says, "Wisdom is the principal thing; therefore get wisdom: and with all thy getting get understanding."

AH'M FROM TEXAS... CAPITOL OF THE U.S.A !

AMERICA, THE 'HENGED'

The summer solstice is celebrated in Salisbury, England, on the Stonehenge reservation. This summer some alleged descendants of the Druids held forth in what they deemed a proper pagan celebration of the sun's ecliptic course but which came closer to the antics of a hard-rock video group. This was done under the eyes of the police, who arrested their normal quota.

Now while the United States can claim its fair share of pagans, it can't seem to come up with a decent summer solstice. It might help if the US had a Stonehenge. The real Stonehenge was built between 10,000 and 12,000 years ago, and it is unlikely Americans are going to stumble on something like it on their side of the Atlantic.

An attempt to remedy this deficiency has been made out near Alliance, Neb., where James Reinders is building a "carhenge" on four acres of his wheat field. As the name implies, it is made up of the chassis of 20 old cars and a discarded ambulance, set

MY WIFE, VI, THINKS THIS ONE OF THE STUPIDEST THINGS I'VE EVER DONE.

on end in a circle rising 11 feet in the air, with spacing identical to Stonehenge. So far as I know, there are no Druids in Nebraska, and Mr. Reinders attributes no religious or astronomical significance to his undertaking.

In fact, he says apologetically that there are no huge stone monoliths lying around in that part of the country—but what it does have is plenty of derelict cars. And like builders throughout the ages, one uses the materials that come to hand. Some Nebraskans think it is a scenic horror. The sheriff of Box Butte County has investigated complaints and, while he finds the results ugly, he did not find them illegal.

Surveying his work, Reinders says: "My wife, Vi, thinks this is one of the stupidest things I've ever done." Maybe so, but before Reinders's effort, America had no henge at all—and no country should be left completely unhenged.

APOLOGIES OF THE ABJECT SORT

Unlike all the rest of the news media, which never make a mistake, the "Lightly" column can come up with some gems of misinformation. This is a humble retraction of some mistaken facts.

Not long ago this column stated the United States didn't have a Stonehenge and therefore the "Carhenge" out in Nebraska, made of old automobiles, was filling a great need. The column also asserted that because of the lack of Stonehenges, there were no druids to have orgies and to chant religious rites in the proper fashion.

Alas! Letters and phone calls have been coming in telling me the US is full of Stonehenges. Well, maybe not *full* of them, but there are enough to turn my face red. They are not of the 10,000-year-old variety such as England can turn out (the earliest in America is circa 1914), but they do exist. They are scattered around in such places as the states of Washington, Missouri, and New Hampshire, as well as other places claimed by various readers. Apparently none is made of plastic.

And as for druids—they are popping out of the woods all over. Of course they are mostly in California, as they should be, and I venture to say they are not honest-to-goodness druids descended from those ancients who painted themselves blue. Perhaps I had better not assert this as a fact, because as sure as I do, a cult of genuine druids will be discovered tomorrow in South Boston.

When corrections like this have to be made, they are not without side effects.

For instance, I had hoped to do a piece on the Eiffel Tower as a unique city ornament. There is nothing like it in any other city of the world, and certainly the US doesn't have one. But I've lost my nerve.

As soon as I make the point there are no Eiffel Towers anywhere in the US, some gleeful person in a city like Amarillo, Texas, will write to say an oil tycoon has just built an Eiffel Tower in his backyard and has imported French-speaking chorus girls to run the elevator.

It's not an easy life. From now on I'll write only about safe topics, like the superior quality of Iowa corn.

CHICAGOPHY

Not much attention has been paid to the battle going on between Chicago and Los Angeles for the title of the second most populous city in the United States. For the information of recent high school graduates, New York City is first.

Until now, Chicago had felt secure in holding second place. But now it seems Los Angeles has edged up into that position by a meager 36,000 people.

It may not be a fair contest. In the past L.A. has been able to extend its city boundaries to any part of the state in which it could find water, thus capturing large hunks of land containing people. As a result, Los Angeles suffers from crooked borders, whereas Chicago suffers only from crooked politics.

Another cry of foul is sometimes heard: that the big California city might be counting its illegals. Chicago doesn't have illegals in significant numbers, unless there are a lot from Mexico, Cuba, and Haiti who got there by mistake. Black

ONE MIGHT SAY THAT ALL AROUND, CHICAGO HAS HAD THE WIND KNOCKED OUT OF IT

Chicagoans are not illegals, regardless of the arguments of the Chicago City Council. They just don't happen to live on the lake front.

But it is no fault of black Chicagoans that the city has seen some dark days. It began its somewhat dubious reputation back when city engineers reversed the flow of the Chicago River, thus pulling the plug, so to speak, on Lake Michigan. There are still some people in Milwaukee who insist it is only a matter of time before all the water in the Great Lakes runs down the Mississippi into the Gulf of Mexico.

Not only has Chicago lost second place in population; according to the weather bureau it has lost first place in claiming to be the nation's windiest city. One might say that all around, Chicago has had the wind knocked out of it.

But the contest is far from over. Chicago may still come up a winner—people are beginning to notice that it has cleaner air than Los Angeles since the stockyards have moved.

D.C. VACATION DAZE

Nothing is going on in Washington right now.

News like this can't be all bad. It is a known fact that less goes wrong in Washington when nobody is there. This is not just one of those sayings of Calvin Coolidge; it is a known fact.

Congress is on vacation until late July. This doesn't mean that some members won't put in a bill for a business trip. Even though this is investigated from time to time, it seems business is where the swimming pools are. The President isn't answering his phone these days, which probably means he is having a barbecue, or out shopping for barbecue sauce.

In other words, Washington is virtually empty. At least the Rev. Jesse Jackson couldn't find anybody to talk with. The only people he has been able to talk with lately, besides Castro, are the 26 Cuban prisoners he brought home with him, and even then a lot is lost in the translation. So Mr. Jackson left town and went to Tijuana. The reason he is hardly ever seen in an American city is that he can act more like a president when he is somewhere else.

Even though the government is at a standstill, everyone says the American economy is still strong. This may simply mean it is strong like a package of Limburger cheese left on the windowsill, but at any rate it is not being tampered with.

Then there are the interest rates. Everyone is talking about interest rates but no one is doing anything about them. Which perhaps is just as well. All we know for sure is that when interest rates went up everyone in the White House left town.

People in the business community keep on saying that the stock market went down only because the prime rate went up. We happen to think the reason the stock market went down is that all the people on Wall Street and in the Federal Reserve System went away on vacation and they don't want any money to be made while they are away. This column predicts the stock market will go up later in the summer when everybody gets back.

Vacation time is all right. But it keeps the budget up. When everyone is away, an entire government payroll has to be added just to answer telephones.

AT LEISURE

52 . . . . MOVIE SCENE

53 . . . . A TAN AT ANY TEMPERATURE

54 . . . . WRITING ON THE SCREEN

55 . . . . FORGET NOT THE ELEPHANT

56 . . . . ROCKY ROADS

57 . . . . SQUOP A WINK

MOVIE SCENE

Every once in a while I go into culture shock. I get a dilettantish feeling of guilt because I stay home and watch TV instead of going out to the movies. Movie people work hard. They pour millions and millions of dollars into making pictures for my entertainment and I hardly ever go. I stay home and either read or absorb TV shows that are not only the pits but appear to be a series of eternal reruns.

This particular night my aesthetic taste rebelled. "What is at the local movie house?" I asked friend wife.

Dutifully she scanned the newspaper. " 'Day of the Dead' is at the Mall No. 1," she said. "The ad shows pictures of skeletons rising up . . . ."

"Never mind. What's at Mall No. 2?"

" 'Teen Wolf.' I think it's about werewolves in high school." In my day we never had werewolves in high school, so I urged her to look further. She did.

"What is 'Mad Max Beyond Thunderdome'?" she innocently asked.

"Some kind of wild superman shooting up cars on the highways," I said, joining her newspaper search. "Here, do you want to see 'Rambo, First Blood'? That's Sylvester Stallone with his shirt ripped off, killing people with a submachine gun and hand grenades."

"He hasn't had his shirt on since 'Rocky I,' " said friend wife. "He probably does it to save on laundry. Oh . . . what's at the new theater?"

" 'Frightnight,' " I said, "and 'Godzilla.' 'Frightnight' is about some terror stalking a neighborhood just like ours. And 'Godzilla' . . . ."

"I know Godzilla. He eats people."

"He doesn't wear a shirt, either," I said. "Here's something called 'The Exterminator.' He kills people with a sawed-off shotgun. But he has his shirt on."

"No. Anything else?"

" 'Return of the Living Dead.' This ad shows some half-skeletons, sort of hovering . . ."

"No thanks." A pause. "What's on television?" I picked up the TV section.

" 'Love Boat,' " I said.

There was an even longer pause.

"Oh well," she said. "I'll put some pizza in the microwave."

A TAN AT ANY TEMPERATURE

Some describe happiness as a northerner in Florida.

During a recent Florida cold snap, I wrapped up in a jacket and muffler to walk to the bank. On the way I met a couple in shorts, T-shirts, and $65 "running shoes" coming in the opposite direction. They were blue around the lips and knees but seemed happy; they stopped to chat, asking where to buy a newspaper.

"Great weather," the man said. "Really great."

"It's only 52 degrees," I said.

"Ha-ha, I guess that's right," the man said.

His pleasant little wife joined the conversation with a shiver of delight.

"It was 20 below when we left Minnesota. This is just great." Chatter, chatter.

When I got to the bank I met a fellow Floridian, wrapped in a woolen sweater and leather gloves. "The ice age cometh," he assured me.

"I just met some people from Minnesota . . ." I began.

"Don't tell me Minnesota. My brother from Canada is visiting me. I just dropped him off at the beach! Canadians are borderline cases," he said.

"Maybe he left two feet of snow up there."

I WOULDN'T CALL IT A TAN.. YOU'RE MORE BLUE

"That's no reason to act like he was in a sauna bath."

I did my banking and walked homeward on the road near the beach where I met a family of four in brand new swimsuits. The plumpish father-type was passing out cones to shivering children. The only thing whiter than his skin was the vanilla ice cream.

He stuttered "hello," so I said, "You must be from Michigan."

"How did you know?" he said. "We're surprised the beach isn't more crowded."

"That's because the temperature is only 52," I told him.

"Oh really?" said his rather husky wife who was probably the same shade of white under her bluish tinge. "We want to get a tan before we go home 10 days from now."

"Ten days ought to do it," I said.

"Anyway there is an exercise club over on the trail with sun lamps."

There is a determination of happiness among northern tourists. They must know the weather is cold but don't want to admit it when they get back home.

Or maybe it isn't happiness at all and the northern tourist is a predictable animal not unlike Pavlov's dogs. He starts taking off his clothes and eating oranges as soon as he sees a row of palm trees.

WRITING ON THE SCREEN

Screenwriters are now hard at work again, according to various happy announcements read on TV.

Many even editorialize and say it is good news.

When writers first went out on strike the TV news pictures showed thousands of writers milling around, holding up printed signs, evidently to prove they could write. But it was not the signs, it was the large number of people in the scene which shook me.

Up until then I had the impression all the scripts on television were written by one person. Television, I believed, couldn't exist without hundreds of duplicating machines lining the corridors outside of network offices.

Now I think it's possible I was mistaken. Watching reruns more carefully, I could see that in the car-chase scenes on one show cars generally flipped over to destruction turning left, while on another show they tipped over to the right, showing a clear difference in the concept of car crashes.

I also noticed that in comedies the sofa was in a different place on different shows and that the characters did vary as to the balance of color and ethnic origins. Even some of the situations were different.

Sometimes it was the boy bewildered by events, sometimes the girl, and more often than not the adults—father, mother, neighbor, or whatever. And, of course, the viewers.

No doubt the trouble is with me.

Throughout my early experience I suppose I knew 50 writers, but they were all out of work most of the time. They didn't strike because they couldn't see how they could make any money unless someone wanted what they wrote. They even dreamed of one day being exploited.

Evidently that's all changed.

And I'm glad the screenwriters are back at work again, even though I don't fully understand unions for writers or the tactics of artistic coercion.

I used to think writers were like cooks. If the food didn't taste good nobody ate it. But cooks have unions now, too.

Come to think of it, so do women. So does everybody.

Maybe I'll have to join something soon.

FORGET NOT THE ELEPHANT

There are so many tensions in the world today that even the reassuring news that the circus has come to New York makes us slightly nervous. Actually, we shouldn't blame world tension. The circus always makes us nervous.

There are a lot of good things about the circus: aerialists, trick riders, clowns, and an overall glamorized sawdust magic which fills us with excitement. But we do worry about the elephants.

But the elephants, being so mighty and yet so massively tolerant with the indignities they have to put up with, make us especially apprehensive, not only about them but about ourselves. There is something terribly ominous about the fact that crowded, noisy, gas-fumed city streets have become the natural home of elephants.

Seeing elephants plodding along 34th Street doesn't make anyone laugh or shout for joy. The pachyderms scuff along, ponderously, huge, incongruous, embarrassed, and sad. Like prisoners on display. And we, in turn, get sad watching them.

What are the feelings of an elephant on 34th Street? He can't relate to it. He doesn't live anywhere in the neighborhood. He doesn't shop at Macy's. Certainly he isn't there to get a laugh. How can anyone laugh at him? New Yorkers are not even afraid of an elephant. They are just casually sad and a little irritated at the traffic jam.

A dog at the end of a leash on Madison Avenue can, on occasion, show some sign of frustrated joy with a bark, a jump, a wag of tail. But an elephant? That represents 25,000 sad, unwagging, unbarking dogs all rolled into one.

At the end of his dusty, tedious march he will be prodded into standing on his head or hind legs and then get some peanuts.

Mostly, people call him Jumbo, a generalized name like others reserved for minority groups, showing small respect. Yet he is the largest four-footed animal in the world, and still he accepts the mad cacophony of 34th Street without a protest.

And speaking of protest: there are plenty of protest marchers everywhere carrying signs to save the whale. But not the elephant. Evidently the elephant is already saved. Maybe if the whale had four legs he might be "saved" too and would be marching along 34th Street behind the elephant.

It wasn't the law of nature that made the elephant what he is. It was us. For our part we hope that we ourselves will never come to this; that we will never know what it is like to be an elephant in New York.

ROCKY ROADS

> WELL... THAT'S THE FOURTH ROCK...

Believe it or not, there are some news items more upsetting to me than the latest quotations from the President.

One such item was the announcement of a movie called "Rocky IV." Even presidents only get two terms. One of the great imponderables of my sterling cinema judgment is that movies that I think are real dogs, and should haunt the memory of Thomas Edison forever, always turn out to make $100 million. Probably this should tell me something. But so far it isn't enough to make me question my own judgment; it's simply annoying that the taste of millions has become suspect.

When I first heard about "Rocky IV" on television, I thought it was the beginning of a comedy hour. Then I realized the commentator was serious. The idea that another heavy-lidded "Rocky" would once more stagger to center ring with puffy lips, glistening all over with a sweaty shine, no doubt made possible with the application of a gallon of salad oil, sent me back to Channel 16 and a rerun of Errol Flynn.

In a battered world where it seems every 10th person gets hijacked, maybe a "Rocky IV" is what we need. It is like a Tom and Jerry cartoon where the good guy is sure to win. To find out why millions are dancing on their toes in anticipation of stuffing more money into the pockets of Sylvester Stallone, I've even thought of getting a computer. Or maybe the computer would suggest that people just go see "Rocky I" four times.

"Rocky I" was about an unknown heavyweight contender. "Rocky II" was his life as a champ and his narrow victory over Apollo Creed, the champ of the previous picture. A guy with a name like Apollo Creed was sure to lose anyway. "Rocky III" is about Rocky fighting his way back from retirement, beating a dude named Clubber Lang (sounds like a champion bridge player).

Now we have "Rocky IV," in which Rocky is up against a new, young Russian type in a battle for the world championship.

Surely, there can be only one more after this: "Rocky V." That would be where Rocky Balboa becomes president, by reason of a knockout in the last hours of the campaign.

SQUOP A WINK

Few people realize that this year is the 100th anniversary of tiddlywinks.

The game was invented in 1888 by Joseph Assheton Fincher, who apparently has no other claim to fame. And if the game had to be invented, a fellow with a name like Fincher would be the one to do it.

A discussion sometimes arises as to whether tiddlywinks is a game or a sport, because the exercise factor is extremely limited. In fact, the only muscles employed to any extent are the thumb and forefinger in squidging. It is so difficult to classify this game as a sport that no nation ever sends a tiddlywinks team to the Olympics.

It is described by some players as a "mental" game, rivaling chess. Of course one doesn't have to be a graduate of the Massachusetts Institute of Technology to play a game of tiddlywinks, but it does seem to help.

The foremost players are from MIT and Oxford University. In fact, the recognized world champion is Larry Kahn, an MIT

THE ONLY MUSCLES EMPLOYED TO ANY EXTENT ARE THE THUMB AND FOREFINGER IN SQUIDGING.

graduate who lives in Miami.

Mathematicians are especially attracted to the game, and the complicated factors in winning seem to be endless. The intricacies are so mystically described by players that I am amazed children ever dared to play it. Apparently there are levels of tiddlywinks the novice can hardly imagine.

Aside from the challenging complications of the game, much of the appeal may come from the use of ridiculous words such as squidging, double wink bristol, squop, nerdle, and winkers. One evidently finds a certain pride in using the right word.

It has been said by those who play both chess and tiddlywinks that chess is boring by comparison. One strategic move in tiddlywinks can change the outcome of a game.

Potting a wink is a main goal, but not the only way of winning. At game's end a wink in the pot is worth three points, while a wink still unsquopped is worth one.

Happy squidging.

BIG BUCKS

60 . . . . FUNNY MONEY

61 . . . . APRIL IS A TAXING MONTH

62 . . . . NOTHING VENTURED, NOTHING OWED

63 . . . . BROTHER, CAN YOU SPARE A TRILLION?

64 . . . . GOVERNMENT CAN BE TAXING

65 . . . . LIVING LIKE A SHEIKH

66 . . . . TROVE, ANYONE?

67 . . . . ONE-LOVE FOR TAX REFORM

FUNNY MONEY

Where spending money is concerned, Americans are unbalanced. They can balance a checkbook, but not a budget. Americans don't worry about a balanced budget but the rest of the world does.

To an American, money is terribly important only when a lunch bill is 38 cents over the cost. He can go into a tirade worthy of TV's J. R. Ewing of "Dallas." But having a $2 trillion federal debt causes him no more concern than fleas on someone else's cat.

If television can be believed, US coastal waters are teeming with Soviet sailors jumping ship looking for asylum. But once ashore they beg to go back to the Soviet bloc. Possibly because they find out about the $2 trillion debt and believe it to be real money. Could they think that if they become American citizens, they will have to come up with $8,000 to help pay it off?

American ambivalence toward finances goes back to when Congress got sulky and wouldn't raise the debt limit. It was announced that the government would run out of money. It sounded like a scenario for an end-of-the-world sci-fi movie.

Technically, the government did run out of money but nothing happened.

Well, it might have spoiled a few tennis games. Some of the old geezers down at the town courts thought that a government running out of money would be like the 1933 depression days when banks ran out of money—they began to hoard tennis balls. These days Americans don't put many dimes in those little jars beside cash registers for local charities. One tends not to believe in American poverty. But African poverty . . . Americans send millions although no one is sure how much of it gets there.

Whales get money, too. When Humphrey the humpback whale took a notion to swim up the Sacramento River in California, experts said it would be bad for him. Americans all but forgot the Geneva summit to concentrate on Humphrey. Someone even set up a money market account for him. For whatever reason, Humphrey decided to go back into his native, less exciting environment—not unlike the sailor who changed his mind. Total expenses for Humphrey was only $60,000. But in his case it was real money.

APRIL IS A TAXING MONTH

Usually on April 15, at 11:40 p.m., I am staggering, bleary-eyed, into my car clutching my completed income tax return in order to drive to a major post office where, according to rumor, it will get postmarked before midnight. I arrive at the post office lobby, only to find half the population of the city in line inching their way toward the mail slot.

This is when I notice I forgot to put stamps on the envelope. I know there is a stamp machine at the other end of the lobby if I want to lose my place in line. I decide to risk it and dash to the stamp machine, where I discover I don't have any change. By this time, the town clock is bonging midnight in a tone of hilarious laughter.

Being a day late filing my tax doesn't upset me too much, it's being reminded of the fact by my wife every few weeks until the following April.

But this year is different. My taxes are all done in advance. My disposition has improved, and I no longer chase pelicans that knock over the birdbath. I even try to love the Internal Revenue Service, which isn't easy, because it doesn't try to love me back.

> THE MENTION OF THE NEW TAX FORM SETS ME OFF . . . NO ONE WITH LESS THAN A GRADUATE DEGREE IN ADVANCED AMBIGUOSITY CAN EVEN GET PAST THE FIRST PAGE.

I'm still not entirely healed. The mention of the new tax form sets me off. It is advertised as easier to fill out. It may be easier than translating a Sanskrit tablet, or a Chinese proverb dating from the Shang Dynasty, but no one with less than a graduate degree in advanced ambiguosity can even get past the first page.

The last time I was called in for an audit the lady reviewing my case put down my 1040, took off her glasses, and said, "At least you get high marks for originality." I'm not positive, but I think they have my picture on the wall along with nine others under the caption "Ten Most Wanted."

My tax return goes in on time now because in a surge of unbelievable fortune I met a fellow who has a room full of computers and can read IRS dialect as if it were "Dick and Jane." He seems normal, however, in all other respects.

April 15 may find me broke, but I no longer chase pelicans.

NOTHING VENTURED, NOTHING OWED

No one gets anywhere in the American economy until he learns not to spend his own money.

It is much the same in Washington. Any congressman who knows the difference between a junket and a gelatin dessert knows that government isn't accomplishing anything unless it is doing something it can't afford.

The caretaker down at the town tennis courts puts it rather well: "We live in a debt-ridden society because we can't get ridden the debts." Nobody can win an election without going into debt. In fact, nobody can lose an election without going into debt.

Candidates in the Soviet Union have a big advantage over Americans in this regard. Mikhail Gorbachev didn't have to borrow millions of rubles to get people to vote for him. Anyway, who would he borrow them from? And all those splendid fur-hatted fellows who lost the race for Communist Party chief probably still have all their kopeks sewed up in their mattresses.

> **ANY CONGRESSMAN KNOWS THAT GOVERNMENT ISN'T ACCOMPLISHING ANYTHING UNLESS IT IS DOING SOMETHING IT CAN'T AFFORD.**

Oh, they might be out of pocket for a few expensive Kremlin lunches, consisting of the Soviet equivalent of creamed chicken in a patty shell. But nothing worth putting in Pravda.

Russian candidates don't have much margin in which to go wrong. Everything is either forbidden or compulsory. So Russians have learned not to complain; not even about the weather. The weather is so much worse in Siberia.

But in the United States it is harder to tell the losers from the winners. If rumor is correct, Gary Hart was a losing candidate and owes $3.7 million. The fact that he owed so much more than losing candidate John Glenn, who is in debt only $2.8 million, makes him look a bit like a winning candidate. It might even give him ideas he ought to run again.

Debts are getting to be a badge of honor. Only important people have them. If you don't owe anybody any money, the chances are you aren't anybody to begin with.

BROTHER, CAN YOU SPARE A TRILLION?

Once upon a time, and not so very long ago, the word "trillion" was always used facetiously.

Most everyone thought of it as a sort of make-believe word, like zillion, which was uttered to quantify something beyond all belief. "I've got a zillion marbles" was more or less the same as "I've got a trillion marbles."

Many people alive today can remember the time when only astronomers would use trillion seriously. Occasionally they might employ other silly words in a serious way, like decillion, but they were talking about light years, or the speed of a comet, or something like that which didn't affect your weekend in the country. Even the planet Pluto isn't that far away.

If you did happen to read trillion aloud to your spouse, it was in a jocund manner, dealing with the distance of a star, and you would get the expected response of a clicking tongue.

But no one used a word like trillion talking about *money*.

However, Washington, the Disneyland of the news media, has changed all that overnight. Trillion is an acceptable word now. It is the only word which can be used to describe a certain situation. In this case the size of America's national debt.

When our man in Washington mentioned that the deficit was a trillion dollars, we smiled and said, "You're kidding. Trillion is something with at least a dozen zeros after it."

"You're thinking of decillion," he said, "which has 33 zeros. Trillion is a much smaller number with only 12 zeros." Well, we happen to think the number 12 sounds big, even if it's only a shoe size.

Just to be clear about it all, we asked a local financial expert how the United States could pay off the debt, and it seems it borrows on the money. In fact it has to borrow money to pay interest on the money it borrows. Try that on your hometown bank for yourself sometime if you want to hear a stone-faced banker go into hysterics.

"Interest on the national debt will jump 12.7 percent to $144.5 billion next fiscal year," he said. "So I think the government will have to borrow $103.2 billion as a net interest outlay. Does that answer your question?"

It doesn't answer the question, but it sure settles any desire about asking any more.

The next word is quadrillion. Does anyone ever say quadrillion seriously?

GOVERNMENT CAN BE TAXING

Protests against military spending are not new. But now the protesters march to a different—and slightly more relaxed—drummer.

Instead of lying down on a cold, wet road in front of an Army truck carrying missile parts and driven by a hot-rod PFC, the new trend is to plop down on the sofa at home and not pay taxes. Not paying taxes will probably not result in ending the spending so much as extending federal borrowing—increasing the national debt. And guess who pays the interest on that debt?

In Wisconsin, people are on this don't-pay-taxes kick because they don't like the government spending their tax money on weapons. They hope others will follow suit. In retaliation, the government might consider putting them all in jail, but this makes for a dilemma. It immediately puts the protesters on the tax-receiving end, instead of the tax-paying end.

One possible way of settling this dispute is for the President to write one of his nice-chatty letters, assuring them that their specific tax money, instead of going for military hardware, will

MAYBE HONEST TAXPAYERS COULD GET EVEN WITH THE PEOPLE IN WISCONSIN AND STOP DRINKING MILK AND EATING CHEESE.

go into a subsidy for the education of illegal aliens. Nothing could be more peaceful than that.

On the other hand, even this could be a problem. There might be families who didn't approve of spending their tax money to educate the families of border athletes. If this anti-illegal-alien group started withholding taxes—or if people only paid taxes for what they liked—the IRS would have to set up an awfully complicated filing system.

In fairness, we must concede that collecting taxes is a dirty job, but somebody has to do it. We don't mean we are consumed with affection for the IRS. It hasn't done us any good turns lately. And its idea of a penalty for a mistake is so grossly out of proportion to the error made that even if the IRS turns out to be made up of people, it may still tend to have its fangs showing.

Solutions are hard to come by. Maybe honest taxpayers could get even with the people in Wisconsin and stop drinking milk and eating cheese.

Or maybe take a drastic step: like running the government on less money.

LIVING LIKE A SHEIKH

It must be as confusing to the average reader as it is to us—the story of Saudi Arabian Mohamed al-Fassi, who got arrested for running up a $1.5 million hotel bill in Hollywood, Fla.

Who can digest this sort of news while gulping the orange juice and one egg special on his way to work? At this rate, isn't it cheaper to buy your own hotel?

The last time we stayed at a motel the bill was $33.86. We had to pay in advance. Not only that but we had to put down the license number of our car. There was no way we could have run up a bill larger than the cost of a newspaper.

In addition to all this, we understand that Mr. al-Fassi is suing the hotel for $1 billion. Allegedly he claims that he was overcharged about $11,000 a day. That's at the rate of over $458 an hour, day and night, if you want to nit-pick.

We were overcharged recently. A hotel restaurant put four soups on our bill when we had only three—an overcharge of $1.75. We didn't go to court over it. Fortunately the waiter remembered his mistake when he was shown that only three of us had spots on our shirts.

One of the most bizarre items in all this was an unpaid cab bill of $157,000. The trip from our last hotel to the airport in a cab cost $8.55. I remember it clearly, the driver wanted his money! We wonder how anyone could ride $157,000 worth before he had to pull out his wallet.

Certain other aspects are remarkable. When we call a hotel for a reservation they don't always have a room. At least they seldom have a room at the rate they advertised. Other times, the room is out in back somewhere next to the soft drink and ice machines which seem to work all night. But in this case Mr. al-Fassi rents three entire floors of a hotel. If hotels have whole floors that are empty, how is it we have such a hard time getting a decent room?

Reportedly, the sheikh has spent about $90 million in Florida over the last couple of years. We are not sure this is true, since we have not seen any of it around our neighborhood. But we live in hope because the taxes are coming due.

With this glimpse of the good life we may try to live our own a little fuller. Maybe at our next hotel stop we will let it be known, discreetly, that we are heir to a $6 billion oil fortune and see how far we can go. The only trouble is, we may not have the nerve to go for the $90 room.

TROVE, ANYONE?

One news item that seems to cheer everyone these days is the treasure find off the Florida Keys worth $400 million. It certainly has cheered treasure hunter Mel Fisher, who announces he is at last rich. And I suppose it cheers me in some perverse way, even though I am not the treasure-finding type.

For most people, finding treasure is a lifelong dream. For me the dream is slightly tarnished ever since I did find a small treasure at the age of seven. Maybe when I say I found a treasure I am using the wrong word.

I had been reading "Treasure Island" for the first time, so for many days I was living out the story. I searched empty lots; I went looking for lost maps in empty houses, and I even carried a small compass around with me, just in case. This haphazard hunting may sound like a hopeless enterprise, but persistence did finally win out. After about a dozen digs in various places, I hit pay dirt. It was buried treasure all right, only 15 inches below the surface in a vacant lot.

My fortune consisted of silvery-looking objects in the form of six forks, five table knives, one large bent spoon, one dented napkin ring with flowery decoration, and a fancy mug with a broken handle. Also, oddly enough, there was a buffalo nickel.

I put the bulk of my treasure in a sack, hid it in my backyard and then went to the store and bought some ice cream with the nickel.

It is hard to explain, but the treasure grew to have a life of its own, which means I kept it for several years, delaying that moment when I could turn it into cash.

The day of decision finally came. I toted the sack down to a jeweler my family knew for an appraisal and possible settlement. Alas, it wasn't silver. In fact, it was appraised as worthless. The jeweler even told me I would have done better throwing the knives and forks away and saving the nickel.

How true. It was only an ordinary buffalo nickel then— dated 1913—but if I had saved it until now it would be a real treasure.

ONE-LOVE FOR TAX REFORM

As far back as I can remember, tax reform was like the weather: Everyone talked about it but nobody did anything about it.

Up until this month I thought the first thing Congress would undertake to reform would be the weather, since compared with taxes it seemed the simpler alternative. But no! Even though the weather has been fairly unpopular with those in the lower income brackets, Congress took on taxes. What this means, in the normal way of Washington, is that it will be another 40 years before we can expect anything to be done about the weather.

Down at the town tennis courts, everyone seems to think that when the final tax bill is passed it will favor the Senate version, so they all expect to be in the 15 percent bracket and have enough money left over to buy tennis balls. Well, there is one fellow who never seems to get a suntan, and who allows he might be stuck in the 27 percent bracket. But he plays with a magnesium tennis racket which probably cost him $250. He also has such a snappy tote bag that all the benches had to be painted because they looked so shabby when he set his bag on them.

It should be pointed out that the gang at the town tennis courts is not made up of typical taxpayers. They really don't *care* if the interest on an IRA will be taxable. They have already been on pension plans so long they are more familiar with initials like WPA.

They would rather have the tax form simple than complicated with investment loopholes. They like to have deductions in round numbers. Personal exemption should be a nice even $2,000 instead of a lopsided $1,080. Standard deductions, joint, should naturally be $5,000 instead of a screwy amount like $4,800. Maybe this is because tennis scoring is in round numbers, like 15, 30, 40, and game. They would hate it to be 15, 32, 47, and game.

I think I go along with the tennis crowd, preferring the Packwood package. But there is no telling what will finally evolve. They have talked about giving the middle-income families a break before this and it never worked out; therefore I rejoice with some trepidation and reservation.

It could be that we all have more faith in the weather.

CHOWING DOWN

70 . . . . THE SOPHISTICATED CANDY COUNTER

71 . . . . FOOD FOR THOUGHT

72 . . . . GRAIN OF HOPE

73 . . . . BEAN GUM SYNDROME

75 . . . . GASTRONOMIC RUTS

THE SOPHISTICATED CANDY COUNTER

While shopping in the supermarket the other day, I stopped at the candy section. I don't do this often, because I don't easily recognize candy anymore.

For one thing, children no longer gathered around the candy display. Candy has become an adult commodity. The packaging, the size, the price, as well as the advertising slant on television, are for a grown-up market. Candy is for the tired housewife or the construction worker who needs a hearty chunk of something to tide him over on the job.

Once upon a time children bought candy at the "candy" store, or "school" store (usually found near the grammar school), where tantalizing sweets could be selected from a display case and acquired for a penny or so. A nickel for candy was nothing less than an orgy.

Unlike the supermarketing techniques of today, candy was unsophisticated. Candymakers were old-fashioned and had the naive idea that candy was for the eight-year-old, appealing to their income bracket as well as their imagination.

Of course this was in simpler times, before people went around poisoning food on the shelves and before the Food and Drug Administration saw the sanitary necessity of putting everything in three layers of plastic. Candy was enticingly unwrapped. For 1 cent a kid could buy long strips of paper with little candy pellets pasted on it, which were bitten off one by one. There were little wax bottles with syrup inside. One could bite off the top and drink the syrup, or one could chew the whole mess together.

In addition there were sour balls, "red hots" (jawbreakers with a hot center), snowballs, 1 cent Tootsie Rolls, and a gelatinous chewy candy made in the shape of coins or "babies." Licorice "whips" were also a cent, as well as a sugary confection in a teeny-weeny tin pie plate which was eaten with a teeny-weeny tin spoon. One can still buy those little multicolored hearts with "Oh you baby" or "Be my Valentine" printed on them, but not in the penny-a-scoop category. The selection went on endlessly.

As I said, I stopped in front of the candy counter recently and hardly recognized it. I did get a package of beautifully wrapped candy bars for $1.40. The package had listed all the calories and daily requirements of thiamine, niacin, iron, etc., as well as about 15 ingredients. I eat only sophisticated candy now.

FOOD FOR THOUGHT

I HAVE BEEN AWARE FOR SOME TIME THAT A LOT OF FOOD DOESN'T HAVE ANY TASTE.

Today's eggs are not what they're cracked up to be.

While following my wife through the aisles of a supermarket behind a grocery cart, feeling like one of the cans people tie behind a "Just married" sign on the bumper of a car, I stopped to eavesdrop on a group talking beside the section containing cartons of eggs.

"Is it me, or is it the eggs?" a white-haired lady in Florida-type slacks was saying. "They have no taste. It's like eating a picture cut out of the food section."

"I know what you mean," said another W.H.L., also in F.T.S. "I have to put minced parsley in Walter's scrambled eggs."

All the other ladies agreed, as well as one small, round gentleman in knee-length shorts, who must have been Walter.

The conversation pleased me. I have been aware for some time that a lot of food doesn't have any taste. Hamburgers today taste like a cardboard box. I do not eat cardboard boxes of course—it's just a figure of speech.

The same problem exists with corn, beans, and bread. Especially bread. I know a lot of people who remember the wonderful, yeasty taste of bread. So, in fear that I was losing my rationality, I recently spoke to an old-time restaurant worker.

"Nowadays people don't *want* things to have taste," he assured me. "If something has a taste they think it's spoiled. Take cheese. It has to taste like *nothing*. Our most popular cheese you can't tell from bean curd."

"I rather miss the taste of food," I said.

"Well," he said brightly, "we have solved that. What we don't have in actual food taste we make up in the way items are described in the menu. Stuff like 'Gourmet's delight, savory poularde à la Neva in succulent sautéed peppers.' It sounds like it has flavor, so no one notices it tastes like boiled hominy."

It's no more a matter of taste, but of education. Walter's still right about the eggs—they need something.

GRAIN OF HOPE

American farmers are happiest when they are selling grain to the Soviet Union. This is because they have an endless amount of trouble making money selling grain to the United States.

Selling grain to the Soviet Union has become the patriotic thing to do, and there aren't very many ways to be patriotic these days and still get paid for it.

Nevertheless, everyone has a slightly uneasy feeling about doing something nice for the Russians. It seems like one is letting the President down. Selling computer chips to the Russians doesn't seem to make some Republicans feel guilty, but it doesn't have that wholesome, generous, patriotic aspect of feeding others.

A farmer selling grain to the Russians gets a feeling of satisfaction. Something like Timex showing the Swiss how to build a watch.

Practically all of the Soviet Union is farmland, but they can't grow anything on it. Either it is too far north, or the rivers all run the wrong way, or the system is basically counterproductive. Yet the Kremlin works day and night (mostly nights) to make the

> ## A FARMER SELLING GRAIN TO THE RUSSIANS IS LIKE TIMEX SHOWING THE SWISS HOW TO BUILD A WATCH.

Soviet farmer happy. He gets booklets, programs, and an eight-hour workday. On the other hand, the only contact the government in the United States has with its farmers is when they try to auction off their farms to pay back the loans. This latter system seems to work better. It makes the farmers tough and they produce wheat.

Even then, Washington looks upon America's grain production as a nuisance. Usually there is no place to put it. It may even come as a surprise to the administration that the Russians would want it.

The American farmer has one other thing going for him. He feels relaxed about the arms race. Secretly he is convinced that the last thing the Russians would want to do is bomb the fields that give them wheat. Since the main diet in Russia is bread, and not caviar, this may make profound sense.

Anyway, the United States farmer is happiest when he is selling grain to the Soviet Union. He can be a Republican and not feel guilty.

BEAN GUM SYNDROME

Lately, I have been noticing food packages.

Over the years a longer and longer list of ingredients has appeared on labels in addition to the main foodstuff in the container. Sometimes this runs to more than two dozen names. This trend indicates to me the growing importance of side ingredients and the decline in the main product one is supposed to be buying.

We may eventually buy our food on an entirely different basis. I see the day coming when the supermarket will sell cans of chemical additives as if they are main dishes, with a little bit of food as flavoring. On the bottom of the label there will be the words "Flavored with chicken noodle soup." I can visualize a section of canned goods labeled only "thiamine." If one reads far enough down the list on the can he will find, near the bottom, "2 percent chow mein noodles."

One of the weirdest lists of extras may be found on a package of cottage cheese. In addition to the cheese, I was somewhat startled to read I was also eating "locust bean gum."

Other things, like lactic acid, I more or less understood, but the locust bean gum took me longer to digest, figuratively speaking.

I suppose eventually natural foods will give place to chemical processes, producing a product that is guaranteed to keep you thin and will deny you all the yummy stuff that makes things taste good.

It is too bad that real food, which we have been eating for thousands of years, is no good anymore. We now have to eat things compounded with chemicals that are either good for you, or good for the economy, it's hard to tell which.

In the days to come when someone asks, "What did you have for lunch?" one's answer will have to be something like, "Well, I had a cup of ascorbic acid, tomato soup flavor."

But all is not lost. I can still look at the list of ingredients on my box of vanilla ice cream. It says only milk, cream, sugar, and natural vanilla. I understand what all of these are. This doubles my enjoyment.

GASTRONOMIC RUTS

Up until a few years ago I thought I was a perfectly normal eater and most everyone else ate funny. My wife—who is also a funny eater—assures me this is not so.

People, over a period of time, get into a gastronomic rut, and to have this pointed out invites either indignation or indigestion. Or both. A lot of people put ketchup on French fried potatoes, but a one-time friend of mine put ketchup on *mashed* potatoes. That is weird by anyone's standards.

In my case, I always suck the pimento out of stuffed green olives before I eat them. If I happen to get a green olive minus the pimento, I have a problem. My wife says I turn the color of the olive, but she exaggerates.

Another thing I do is pull Oreo cookies apart. I eat the plain side first and the frosting side last. When I was accused of being a fuddy-duddy, I tried to change the habit, but it was of no use. I am convinced that is the proper way to eat Oreo cookies.

Why do people break spaghetti before boiling it? This is a sin. Spaghetti should be thin, cooked at full length, and when eaten turned on a fork. Some say short spaghetti tastes the same as

I ALWAYS SUCK THE PIMENTO OUT OF STUFFED GREEN OLIVES BEFORE I EAT THEM.

long spaghetti, which is nonsense—a falsehood perpetrated by spaghetti-breakers.

Hot should be hot and cold should be cold. Some restaurants serve water without ice and soup lukewarm. In fact, soup and water come at about the same temperature, if not the same consistency. Waiters look shocked when I ask for colder water and hotter soup.

Steak should be eaten rare or not at all. This is sometimes difficult. While one can send back soup to have it heated, it is more difficult to send back a steak and have it rarefied. Here I have some reluctant flexibility, unless the steak appears looking like a burnt gym shoe.

Oleo is a special pet peeve. I am horrified when I order buttered toast at breakfast and it comes oleoed instead. Soaked and slathered. But worst of all is a glob of oleo floating on top of a bowl of oyster stew.

I think the word "garni" should be eliminated from all menus. I could go on, but I don't want readers to get the idea I have funny eating habits.

DOWN TO EARTH

78 . . . . BRACKEN CREEP

79 . . . . ASTRO SURF

80 . . . . FINDING FAULT

82 . . . . GARBAGE YARDAGE

83 . . . . NOT FOR THE BIRDS

BRACKEN CREEP

Since the Civil War, the South has had its share of problems.

It is not out of the woods yet. In fact, you can say it is getting deeper into the woods. This is because of kudzu, which some Southerners think is worse than the Union Army.

Kudzu is from Japan, as are a lot of other things these days. It sounds like something a person yells while doing karate, but it actually is a fast-growing vine. Its growth rate, we are told, has been compared with Subaru, another Japanese import, and while it does not move as fast as the car on level ground, it allegedly wins races going uphill. In several undocumented cases, small autos and trucks have lost the race against the kudzu vine and disappeared. Their spare parts, including hubcaps, have turned up later inside kudzu pods.

This tough, vigorous vine was introduced to the United States as a means of controlling soil erosion, especially along steep road embankments. It surpassed expectations. It not only covered the road embankments but also the roads—as well as fences and the occasional gas station.

Floridians and Georgians have extremely strong opinions about the plant. Kudzu, they tell you, is never planted on purpose. But they are careful of what they say if they think the plant is within earshot.

Actually, the ominous, hairy vine is the sort of thing monster movies are made of. With the right director, and Vincent Price as the mad botanist, a kudzu horror movie could gross $125 million. That is, if the actors survived to finish the picture and kudzu got top billing.

Events have now taken a curious turn. Just at the point when people in Florida and Georgia are making a last, gallant stand, sending their children to places where even kudzu can't grow, like North Dakota, a pro-kudzu movement has sprung up in Tennessee. Certain groups are claiming that kudzu not only can be made into baskets and furniture but can also be used as a cheap, fast food, to be eaten with noodles and fried seafood. The taste, a carefully guarded secret among those poor wretches who volunteered for the experiment, presumably could enhance the flavor of squid, eels, or octopus. There are no reports of interest from Burger King.

It is obvious that since it is impossible to control kudzu growth, the US must put it to some expandable use. Either that, or find a way to match kudzu against the fire ant invasion.

ASTRO SURF

Coastal erosion is one of the natural functions going on in the world of geology. Nature seems to be none the worse for it, but it bothers people. Beach types go bonkers over erosion even though it has been around longer than taxes.

It is an obvious act of discrimination against folks who live by the seaside. Thus far it has never occurred to people not to build houses too close to the water, even though the fact that tides and waves cannot be regulated was settled by King Canute back around AD 1020.

The latest coastal-consciousness item on the market is fake seaweed. This comprises strips of plastic grass, four feet wide, stuck in long rows off the coast and held in place by sandbags. Not a very remarkable idea, but when one thinks of the length of inhabited coastline it boggles the mind. So far, no one is absolutely sure whether the fake sea grass will build up the sand and prevent erosion.

Officials always approach something as absurdly expensive as this with an open mind. It is sure to mean money in the pockets of somebody, even though it comes out of the pocket of someone else. Presumably, plastics manufacturers, who gave us

> **TURTLES ARE PERHAPS THE ONE SPECIES LESS KEEN WITTED THAN SEASIDE DWELLERS.**

AstroTurf, would be in favor of it.

As always, in the normal course of politics, there is a diversity of opinion. Although some have a fair amount of confidence in how the seaweed barrier will affect the shoreline, no one is sure how it will affect the turtles.

Turtles, as a look at one plainly tells, are borderline cases to begin with. They are perhaps the one species less keen witted than seaside dwellers, and might not know the difference between real grass and plastic grass. At times of the year they can be as stubbornly beach-committed as their human counterparts. A frequent diet of plastic grass might eliminate the turtle population once and for all.

In some areas, turtles have been known to eat plastic already. Not grass. Presumably just plastic bananas, apples, and whatnot, used for decoration and finally cast into the sea.

The outcome seems inevitable. Once all this plastic grass is in place, weighted down with sandbags, there will be nothing to do but put in plastic turtles.

Either that, or quit building houses on the beach.

FINDING FAULT

Recently we have become concerned about cracks in the earth.

Although we have been assured by people in very high places that there is nothing to worry about, we feel that cracks in the earth are not a good thing. They certainly are bad when they appear in skyscraper foundations, in bridges and in the engine block of our automobile.

So why are cracks in the earth's crust reported only on the back pages of a newspaper or on midday educational television?

While it is true that these cracks have been here for a long time (some say 200 million years) no one seems to take them seriously. People talk and talk about the earth cracking up but no one does anything about it.

Maybe it is understandable. After all, the cracks don't show. Mostly they are in the middle of the Atlantic Ocean, or somewhere out of sight in the Pacific or Indian Oceans. If they were in the vicinity of Pennsylvania Avenue in Washington, DC they would get attention soon enough. From the Democrats, anyway.

These cracks and crevasses may be evidence of continental drift, and we are against continental drift. Continents, we believe, ought to stay where they are.

It is quite possible that the fear of drifting continents is responsible for much of the illegal immigration into the United States. If people get too worried that the place where they live is drifting into trouble they naturally will want to go live in some more steady place. The United States seems to be one of those stable areas, which may sound funny to anyone who watches television.

Not that the cracks in the crust don't touch the United States. They do. But the only important crack in America is the San Andreas fault, which runs from north to south in the vicinity west of the Sierra Nevada mountains. The worst that could happen as a result of this crack would be for California to drift out into the Pacific Ocean and sink, a result which many believe would not be entirely negative.

But it is not the cracks in the earth, per se, which concern us. It is the psychological effect on the inhabitants who live atop them. They would be prone to crack-up thinking.

California may or may not be a good illustration but from the study of geodetic charts one can see that serious cracks run through the Mideast, through Iran, and up into the Asian areas of the USSR. Then there is one from the Kamchatka Peninsula down into Southeast Asia.

All potentially jittery areas, now, and in time to come.

We feel something should be done. Maybe it is too much to expect they could fill up the affected areas with cement but, on the other hand, we can't stand idly by and watch the world crack up. Especially when we don't know whose fault it is going to be.

GARBAGE YARDAGE

For more than two months a garbage scow, with a crew equipped with gas masks, has towed 3,100 tons of garbage around the Western Hemisphere hoping to find a country needing this sort of product.

There seems to be very little demand for garbage these days. The cargo has been refused by Long Island, North Carolina, Alabama, Mississippi, Louisiana, Texas, Florida, Mexico, Belize, and the Bahamas—even though a lot of these places might have absorbed the garbage and no one would have known the difference.

Prejudice is not dead, apparently, as to what ruins a neighborhood. Anyway, according to reports, 27 states claim to have all but run out of space to put garbage in. This certainly applies to New Jersey.

In the old days garbage wasn't such a problem. Take auto tires, for instance. When they were worn out, they were put out on the front lawn and flowers planted in them or else tied to a tree for a swing. Maybe similar inventive things could be done today with other garbage, like plastic bottles, grapefruit rinds, and chicken bones.

It is deplorable, but America seems presently to have an excess in qualities of personal indulgence over other countries. The US generates more garbage per person, more academic ignorance, more teen-age pregnancy, and shoddy workmanship. Perhaps these characteristics are related.

Japan is a country only about the size of California with 121 million people. Yet its garbage problem is under control. This is because the Japanese create only half as much garbage per person, recycle more of it, and turn the rest into energy. It is also possible they ship some to the US. It may or may not be true that Toyotas are made out of recycled Pepsi-Cola cans.

Americans, being pragmatic Democrats, often zig when they should be zagging. Probably they shouldn't have tacked that statement onto the pedestal of the Statue of Liberty: "Give me . . . the wretched refuse of your teeming shore . . ."

Everyone suddenly has enough refuse. What we all need now is reclamation.

THERE'S A BETTER CLASS OF GARBAGE IN NEW JERSEY

NOT FOR THE BIRDS

Hardly anyone can deny the environment is in some kind of trouble.

The reason it is in trouble is that it is too much like one of those pottery piggy banks. You can't get any money out of it unless you ruin it. And anyone who isn't after money is highly suspicious in the eyes of administrative Washington today. That puts environmentalists on the endangered lists along with the rest of the wildlife.

Inside Washington an environmentalist is acceptable if he goes to Tarzan movies and watches Jacques Cousteau on television. Outside Washington an environmentalist seems to be anyone who doesn't work for the Environmental Protection Agency. America's biggest challenge in the coming years will be to outlast the EPA.

According to some sources, President Reagan's education in environmental history came from acting in westerns. If this is true, he could always point to the movies of American Indians as an example. They supported the environment and look what happened to them.

The news media sometimes hint that the President isn't in favor of supporting the environment at all; but this can't be true. When environmentalists were demanding he fire Anne Burford from the EPA, what was his response? He said he is "not going to

> **INSIDE WASHINGTON AN ENVIRONMENTALIST IS ACCEPTABLE IF HE GOES TO TARZAN MOVIES AND WATCHES JACQUES COUSTEAU ON TELEVISION.**

run for cover and throw someone off the sleigh." How can anyone who rides around in a sleigh with Anne Burford be against the environment? In case some readers don't know what a sleigh is, it is a horse-drawn vehicle with runners for carrying people over the snow. You can't get closer to nature than that.

When the President is not riding in a sleigh, he is riding a horse. You need some kind of environment for a horse. Presumably Ronald Reagan chose the location of his California ranch because it is a high-class environmental property without any factories next door. It isn't even situated on the site of a chemical waste dump. It may be one of the few places that isn't.

Anyway, it shows his heart is in the right place and with all those trees and hills around him it is no wonder he thinks people who worry about the ecology are extremists.

Extremists are hard to define. Naturally, it depends on where your ranch is. But these extremists, President Reagan says, won't "be happy until the White House looks like a bird's nest."

Offhand, this doesn't seem likely, even if some birds did dare to build a nest on the White House. Probably the White House is sprayed every so often just to prevent this kind of takeover.

After all, who would want it to be said that this administration is for the birds?

NOTES ON NOISE

87 . . . . NO SILENCE, PLEASE

88 . . . . MUSICAL SLEEPERS

89 . . . . LESSIBLE DECIBELS

No SILENCE, PLEASE

Commercial telephone conversations have obviously undergone serious scientific study since the days when people just got busy signals. Our psyches have been computerized.

Business houses no longer trust our naked, unprogrammed decisions. They feel we no longer know what we want or like until we have been thoroughly probed by IBM.

Evidently it has been discovered that nobody can stand silence on the telephone anymore. It is now thought that silence frightens us to the point that we either hang up or say we don't want any.

As a result, when we make a phone call and don't get an immediate connection, the corporation we are calling puts us on "hold," and while we wait woos us with soothing music. Well, music may be too specific a term. It is a sound imitating music. It is a xylophone-violin version of "The Blue Danube" or else a tight little female voice singing, "I hear music when there's no one there. . . ."

If the oncoming business conversation involves more money and greater courage, one might listen to the theme from "Star Wars."

> **A DOZEN YEARS AGO SOME MEDDLESOME SCIENTIFIC BUSYBODY FOUND OUT THAT COWS GAVE MORE MILK IF THEY LISTENED TO MUSIC.**

This is the direct result of earlier research.

A dozen years ago some meddlesome scientific busybody found out that cows gave more milk if they listened to music. I have never been in a barn where all the cows were contentedly wearing earphones, but a lot of farms did use loudspeakers to pipe in old bovine favorites such as "The Anniversary Waltz."

Cows loved it. Except in barns where Chinese music was used and the milk soured, milk production zoomed.

Apparently the same holds true for people. If one hears sweet music he is likely to give more milk, figuratively speaking, to a company plying him with pseudo-symphonic recordings.

But recently I had a shock. While at a garage I called home for some information about the car. My wife answered. When she heard what I wanted she said, "Just a minute, I'll look it up." And suddenly I was listening to a tinny version of "Home Sweet Home" on my own telephone. I yelled for my wife to turn it off, but she couldn't.

We've got a "hold" button on our *own telephone* which insists on soothing the waiting ear.

MUSICAL SLEEPERS

Hardly anyone talks about snoring. I think that's because most people who snore try to pretend they don't. At least they don't want to be caught at it.

Snoring is no respecter of persons. A tough, unshaven dude may not snore at all, while some sweet, young maiden might peel the paper off the bedroom wall.

To illustrate this, consider a young couple I knew who got married. He was not much to look at but she was a dainty Cinderella. After they returned from their honeymoon, I happened to meet him on the street and made some supposedly humorous remark about enjoying a conjugal bedroom. He made a terrible face.

"She snores," he said, rolling his eyes.

"Well," I said. "That's not so terrible . . . "

"Oh, it isn't just that she snores," he went on. "It's like a circular saw going through a 10-inch plank. I've heard Boeing 727s make less noise on takeoff." Of course they've patched things up since then, although I don't know how. Maybe separate rooms. Or she sleeps with a pillow case over her head.

There have been a few studies made about snoring. Results seem to show that people who sleep on their side snore less than those who sleep on their back. Snore studiers say it's a sort of reed effect, like air going through a pipe organ. Anyway, it's a matter of vibration, although not necessarily harmonic.

In cartoons a "balloon" is put above the character's head with different letter formations to indicate snoring. They range from the simple "ZZZ" to "ZORK" or "KACKKK." Sometimes people wake themselves up snoring but more often they don't. Snoring doesn't make many friends but neither does telling people that they snore.

I think a fortune is to be made inventing a sort of musical instrument that would fit over the sleeper's nose and mouth and that would translate the guttural snore sound into a catchy tune. Like those fancy horns on automobiles.

LESSIBLE DECIBELS

Things don't upset me the way they used to.

When I was a kid I was shaken to learn that my favorite screen idol, Elmo the Mighty, did not really lift an elevator full of imperiled people by himself. He was assisted by a power winch off camera. I also went into a brief decline when I discovered my seventh-grade teacher whose curly blond hair I admired wore a wig. But I was not too much undone by recent information that musicians in symphony orchestras use earplugs.

Oh, I raised an eyebrow, but only because it seems unfair. They expect *us* to listen to the music. After thinking it over calmly, however, I could see that a musician wearing earplugs was not in the same category as someone I know who simply puts his fingers in his ears at concerts. He does it even with soft music.

And earplugs do not come under that crass judgment of the crude critic of opera who says he knows it isn't "over till the fat lady sings."

It can be assumed that symphony musicians have sensitive ears. Orchestras can get awfully loud, especially when they shoot off cannons in the "1812 Overture." Even music in the medium range like the Anvil Chorus from "Il Trovatore" can shake a few pins loose at times. So if an unfortunate musician finds himself somewhere in front of the brass section, or even near that skinny, baldheaded fellow who beats the kettle drums, he is apt to be in for a double dose of decibels.

There is one curious aspect of this earplug thing; a musician isn't required to bring his own earplugs. If he feels he needs them, they must be provided by management. Of course, a musician is supposed to bring his own instrument, but it could be embarrassing for him to be caught carrying around his own earplugs. As if he didn't want to hear his own music.

Eventually something better will be worked out. Through long tradition the public has come to expect a musician to listen to his own music, so if it is too loud, other devices may be used. Plexiglass shields, thick carpets, and more space are being tried.

Rock groups are not discussed, since many suspect that rock musicians go tone-deaf early in their careers and do not actually hear the music they make.

Earplugs for the audience have also been suggested. But this would bring up the old puzzle: If an orchestra plays on a deserted island where there is no one to hear it, does it make a noise?

OUT OF THE DEEP

92 . . . . 'MR. GOOD GUY'

93 . . . . SOGGY KISSES

94 . . . . WATCH A WHALE—AND RISE ON THE SOCIAL SCALE

95 . . . . FISH AREN'T WHAT THEY USED TO BE

'MR. GOOD GUY'

Sharks are in the news again, but it is no more "Mr. Bad Guy" press coverage they are receiving. Articles have been appearing by shark experts and students at marine centers revealing that these denizens of the deep have been misunderstood and maligned. One simply has to know them better. The articles do not offer suggestions on how to do this, but swimming in shark-infested water is not recommended.

Some accounts of their behavior do make them seem a bit like Boy Scouts of the sea, and perhaps it would help to start thinking of them in this way. A shark is trustworthy, a shark is loyal, a shark is helpful, a shark is friendly, and so on.

On top of everything else, they are thought to be quite adaptable. In places where sharks are studied, some have been taught to ring bells. The ringing of a bell is a mark of great friendliness when done by a fish—or even an animal. The fact that it does not hold true in the case of human beings is not necessarily at issue.

There seems, however, to be one great trouble with sharks. No matter how many nice things one says about them, they still look sneaky. They have beady eyes and rows of sharp teeth, and they slither through the dark waters. They have the same mean look they had 100 million years ago, when, as I understand it, there were no good guys. Everybody took a nip out of everybody else just for the sake of evolution. Sharks never got pretty.

Take the porpoise, for instance. One can hardly mistake a porpoise for Miss America until you put it alongside a shark. A porpoise might look like a kind but ugly relative, whereas a shark will always look like someone about to foreclose a mortgage. Friendship has got to be more than sharkskin deep.

Occasionally someone claims to have been chased by a shark! This is hard to credit, sharks being as friendly as they are. But I have a theory. Sharks have a very keen sense of smell. When a person is splashing around offshore he may still be wearing traces of aftershave which send alluring vibrations through the water. Or maybe it's an exotic perfume with a fetching name like Midnight Madness that playfully tweaks a shark's snout.

Perhaps instead of maliciously attacking a swimmer, the shark merely wants to bask in the latest smell sensation from Paris.

IF YOU CAN'T LOOK SMART, LOOK MEAN

Soggy Kisses

Almost anywhere in Florida or California, one is able to visit a sea world, sea circus, or sea-something, in which man and beast are throwing arms and fins around each other in pledged affection.

In the old days, one just went to an aquarium. There he looked into the sides of a glass tank and only saw stupidly astonished fishes swimming around—noticeably devoid of talent. They never picked up a Frisbee or hugged anybody, and their only accomplishment was an ability never to blink their eyes.

Then later, some places made improvements and had "underwater shows" in which one sat, comfortable and dry, in a theater seat looking through a picture window into the depths of a bubbling spring called something like Kissamahoochie. There he watched a bevy of beautiful girls cavorting in about nine feet of water.

These shows are successful. They would be even more so if the audience could stop holding its breath in sympathy and not go out gasping for air.

But things are changing. The fish and girls have been replaced by intelligent, squeaking dolphins. Giant killer whales have moved in with a great act that soaks the passive spectators with salt water from titanic flip-flops. It is fun on a massive scale. To prove it, the killer whales zoom up and kiss children and elderly ladies on the cheek. In return, ladies and children grab the whale and kiss him on the wet nose. Thus far, a killer whale has not inadvertently yawned at the wrong time.

The trend in finny actors seems to have stopped with whales. An acquaintance of mine, bored with the predictable whale routine, asked when they were going to hire some talented six-ton sharks. The management ignored the suggestion. Apparently killer sharks try harder to live up to their reputation than killer whales, to compensate for their smaller size.

But nothing is impossible. At one time, no one could foresee kissing whales. Probably in the near future someone will put sharks on the program and they will fetch Frisbees and jump through hoops. I'm not sure about the kissing.

WATCH A WHALE—AND RISE ON THE SOCIAL SCALE

WHERE IS EVERYBODY?

One thing in vogue today is whale-watching.

Why so many people want to see whales swim by is not clear, but a lot of coastal boat captains make a big living from this need. Most whales are covered with barnacles, and one sees only the fluke waving about. So as one tourist aptly stated, "When you've seen one whale's tail, you've seen them all."

One reason people give for wanting to see a whale is that they are the biggest animal alive today. But even if they see only a small whale, it apparently satisfies the need to overcome the social stigma of not seeing a whale at all. Anybody who is anybody has seen a whale, and if you are one of the unglamorous people who cannot offhandedly boast of a recent whale sighting, you'd better avoid important social gatherings.

One thing should be explained, however.

Some people mistakenly believe whale-watching includes going to Sea World and seeing Shamu, the "killer whale," do his tricks. This does not, repeat, does not count as whale-watching, and gives no prestige in the social scale. Shamu doesn't even have barnacles, and he lives in a tank. Furthermore, he has lived with people so long that he may not even know he is a whale!

Whales can be found almost anywhere. They are at home in both the Atlantic and Pacific Oceans. One popular spot on the East Coast of the United States is Cape Cod, where there is a Cape Cod Whale Watching Hotline, in case tourists wandering around the vicinity don't know where the whales are.

One can't be too critical of this new fad. Whales are very high on the scale of animal intelligence and live in a rather advanced social order, which includes an underwater language of musical moanings and groanings. If people didn't watch whales, whales might well organize ways to watch people.

Maybe that's what is going on now. Maybe the *de rigueur* thing is not so much whale-watching as it is to be seen by a whale. A real, honest-to-goodness, barnacle-covered whale, that is.

FISH AREN'T WHAT THEY USED TO BE

Have you eaten any shark lately? How about fried mahi-mahi, blowfish, or puffer?

I have tasted shark out of curiosity. If I hadn't known what it was, I would have thought I was eating the rubber mat from underneath the steering wheel of our Buick, with oil spots on it. One might say a shark tastes a good deal the way it looks.

Like many who have lived most of their lives in New England, I have a natural inclination to eat fish. But something is happening to normal fish. Delicacies such as baked halibut, stuffed flounder, and poached mackerel seem to be disappearing, while strange flatfishes with even stranger names are being pushed at us instead. Or else they have no names at all but are offered as "batter-fried fish" or "fish sticks."

Usually there is an effort to hide the thing under a prettier name; thus, when you read "salmon shark" you must translate, "dogfish."

Even high-class restaurants are changing their standards. "What's calimari?" I asked.

"Squid," the waitress replied.

"Why don't they say squid?"

A horrified look. "People might not eat it!"

The United States now imports 70 percent of its fish, just as it imports 70 percent of practically everything else. No wonder once-familiar names, like scrod, have become almost unknown. The big

I THOUGHT I WAS EATING THE RUBBER MAT FROM UNDERNEATH THE STEERING WHEEL OF OUR BUICK

name now is monkfish. One can be happy eating it as long as one never gets a look at it in its natural state.

One day I went into a fish house and asked for some halibut broiled in herb butter and lemon juice. "We don't have halibut," the waiter said; "we have pollock. You can't tell the difference."

Pollock is a fish no one ever heard about a few years ago. Now it is a substitute for everything. Shredded, it passes for crab meat.

Scallops can be made from sea skates by using a cookie cutter, but let's not press this subject too far.

ON OTHER THINGS

99 . . . . A PROBLEM OF PINS AND KEYS

100 . . . . POST OFFICE BLUES

101 . . . . NIGHT VISITOR

102 . . . . ALL LOCKED UP

103 . . . . NEWS FROM THE BULL ELEPHANT FRONT

104 . . . . THERE SHE GOES

105 . . . . FAIR TO MIDDLING

106 . . . . WOBBLING TENNIS BALLS

107 . . . . BIG BROTHERLY LOVE

108 . . . . THE OTHER LAUGH FEST

109 . . . . GOVERNMENT SECRETS

A PROBLEM OF PINS AND KEYS

There are a few problems I haven't solved yet.

The most pressing one at present is what to do with pins I take out of a new shirt.

Something in my upbringing forbids me to throw pins away; besides, where can you throw them? They are like old razor blades.

Our wastebaskets are wicker, or other woven material, so pins that might go into one would never come out again but would lurk there forever waiting to stick somebody.

Usually I take the pins out and put them carefully in a shallow china dish on the dresser.

This tray already has pins from previous shirts going back 10 or 12 years. It also has some hairpins, bobby pins, small buttons, a broken chain to attach to glasses, three rubber bands, and 2 cents. These items will remain for future generations to throw away. No one in the family knows what to do with them.

The inability to throw away pins may date back to that awful saying: "See a pin, pick it up. . . ." And while no one throws pins away, I've seen people pick them up.

I suppose they are added to other piles of pins in other houses. Eventually it will be like the garbage surplus. We will have floating scows full of used pins with nowhere to dump them.

Another great problem I have is suitcase keys.

You can't tie a key to the suitcase handle, because then the key would make no sense. The key can't be put inside the suitcase, because after the suitcase is locked you can't get it out.

In the top drawer of my desk I have a large envelope full of keys that don't fit anything. I keep them because there is always that eternal hope that a key and a lock will take to each other.

Someone is sure to write in and advise me to buy a case with a combination lock, which doesn't need a key.

I have two of these at present which I can't open. I suppose I will remember the numbers one day, which I am sure are written down inside, put there before I locked it.

Meanwhile, what does one do with a locked, empty suitcase?

Lately we have been reduced to traveling with just a shopping bag. It always fits under an airplane seat and everything is instantly available.

We haven't lost all pride, however, since we always try to have a shopping bag from Neiman-Marcus or Saks. Once we did have to make do with a bag from J.C. Penney, but it was just a short trip.

Problems may always be with us, but I haven't given up.

POST OFFICE BLUES

In taking informal polls at the tennis courts, the beach, and the town dump, I find no one loves the post office anymore.

This is too bad, because at one time the post office sort of took care of you and asked how Aunt Carrie was after her trip to the city. And once I had a letter delivered from overseas addressed only to G. Le Pelley, Connecticut. They can't do that today with ZIP codes.

For some reason, the post office seems to hate the business it's in.

Employees stand around frowning at the computerized machines sorting mail. With all this show of efficiency, why does it take up to five days for some letters to travel 300 miles?

Does a postman walk all the way?

I'm not sure such unpopularity is deserved, but the Great Post Octopus goes along unbothered by lack of public love.

For one thing, the organization seems to be big on slogans and very short on solutions. Still, many people vote for politicians who meet that description, so maybe the post office just needs more charisma.

Raising the price of a stamp to 25 cents while giving less service didn't help any.

One still has to lick it himself, and it doesn't taste any better than the old 22-center. On the other hand, the little square piece of paper pays for its airplane ride from New York to San Francisco, so honest value must be seeping through somewhere.

Of course the mail itself isn't what it used to be. My wife brings in four or five pounds of letters from our mailbox and when I ask, "What's in the mail?" she says, 'Nothing."

I don't suppose the post office can be blamed for the impersonal mishmash the mail has become, but people feel the need to blame somebody.

It may be that telephones have taken the urgency out of the postal business the same way they took the excitement out of telegrams. After all, if one talks fast he can call long distance for only a wee bit more than it takes to send a letter, and one gets the answer at the same time.

But nothing stays the same. Advertising and solicitation are taking over the telephone just as they have taken over the mail, so maybe all the post office has to do is sit and wait.

Its time will come again.

NIGHT VISITOR

No one down at the town tennis courts has seen Halley's comet yet—except one left-handed player who claims to have seen it twice, the first time in 1910.

His statement about the comet caused some doubtful indignation, because it was first thought he claimed to have seen it three times, which in terms of years would take some doing. Such a boast was consistent with his character, however, since he tends to exaggerate, especially about past tennis games, including some with Don Budge in high school.

As it turned out, his claim was not about himself but an assertion that his five-year-old grandson will see Halley's three times. His theory is that after the year 2000, space travel will have become so sophisticated that the comet's path could be intercepted, by passenger spacecraft, on its opposite ellipse.

Whether or not people would take space trips of 50 or 100 million miles to get an extra look at a comet, the way they now drive 60 miles to Sea World or Busch Gardens, is a moot point. Especially when astronomers and learned stargazers continually

> **HALLEY'S COMET . . . IS OUR ONLY LOYAL, EVER-RETURNING, FRIENDLY RELATIVE FROM OUT OF THE FAR REACHES OF THE UNIVERSE . . .**

describe it as a "dirty little snowball." It is a sad fact that more and more people are thinking of this visiting phenomenon as a hunk of junk.

Halley's comet deserves better.

It is our hook on the universe. It is our Moby Dick, our Old Faithful, our "man's best friend." It is our only loyal, ever-returning, friendly relative from out of the far reaches of the universe which drops by to say "hello" but never wears out its welcome.

Unlike other unfriendly asteroids and dirty hunks of ice, which crash into Earth with rude inebriation, Halley's flies by with friendly dignity, on astronomically frequent intervals, wagging its tail.

No one down at the town tennis courts has seen Halley's comet yet (with the possible exception of Lefty, the dubious raconteur), but before next spring arrives I hope everyone in the world will have seen it, smiled at it, and wished it well on its long, dark, probing orbit through time and space.

ALL LOCKED UP

Things aren't like the good old days. In fact, maybe they never were.

Security is the obsession of the day. It has become so vital you can reach out and touch someone only on the telephone.

A statement heard almost every day is that no one ever used to lock his door when he went out. For that matter, no one used to lock his car.

Something new is now being said: "Remember when we used to lock just the ignition and the doors of our car?" That is because we now have to lock not only the ignition and the door but also the glove compartment, the trunk, the steering wheel, the hood, the gas tank, at least one front wheel, and also activate a siren alarm which will go off if anyone approaches the car from the wrong direction.

It doesn't seem to help. Every year more cars get stolen.

Even dog collars have locks on them.

We have a friend who lives in the city. The door of his apartment has seven locks on it. Still he has been robbed on two different occasions. Both times through the window. He is now planning on installing bars and electric grids with a pulsating current of 120 volts.

Business establishments have the same problem. A number of gas stations have installed killer dogs at night. This has been a mixed success, since in at least one case the owner himself was unable to get back in for two days. A radio store owner, when questioned, admitted he not only has alarms installed in the main doors and roof but has a cobra sleeping in the window. He also has a large banana spider, but he claims this is only for bugs.

The security obsession has focused a larger interest on guns. It may not be pertinent to security but gold handguns are now being sold in Beverly Hills for $10,000 apiece. These not only differ from the Saturday Night Special in price but can be bought on Sunday after church.

We are not against all that money that is being made by people in the business of security systems. We are just not happy with locks. This is partly because we are always losing the key.

But we have a further unhappiness. The security guards, airport police, and a lot of uniformed patrol people have an unreassuring look. They look exactly like the people we thought we were being guarded against.

NEWS FROM THE BULL ELEPHANT FRONT

Maybe nobody else notices, but news items are getting weird. There isn't much in the news that seems real anymore.

Probably the reason for this is that no one pays any attention to the "straight" news.

There is fighting still going on in Lebanon. I find it no longer has any effect on me. The pictures of bombed-out houses on television could all be reruns from last year.

The continuous arguments about the budget and taxes, now running into the trillions of dollars, have almost no meaning for people like me who struggle to balance a checkbook and come out $7.81 in arrears.

Since primary news has so little meaning, secondary news has taken over.

For instance, the news that really upsets me is an item about a woman who is suing her husband for negligence when she was attacked by an African bull elephant. The operative word here is "negligence." What is required of a person not to be negligent around an African bull elephant?

A WOMAN IS SUING HER HUSBAND FOR NEGLIGENCE WHEN SHE WAS ATTACKED BY AN AFRICAN BULL ELEPHANT

This evidently happened in Africa, but I can't help putting myself in the picture. Elephants are everywhere these days and the size of them remains relatively constant throughout the world. I don't think a lawsuit looms large in my future, but one never knows.

The term "negligent" was not defined by the news item, but it could hardly mean anything less than entirely vacating the scene. If there is any flexibility in the law, it would surely be put to an extreme test in this case.

My position is, the courts ought to allow some latitude in cases like this which might come up from time to time.

If negligent was merely acting out what comes naturally, that's one thing. On the other hand, if the husband was on the sidelines actually cheering for the elephant, that's another. In that case he ought to have the book thrown at him.

Even if he had taken refuge in a tree, there might be some point of law in his favor if he was yelling encouragement to his wife: "Atta girl, Matilda, kick him in the leg!"

It is all beginning to seem just as plausible as Lebanon.

LOOK HIM IN THE EYE, SWEETHEART

THERE SHE GOES

Although Svetlana Savitskaya, the female Soviet astronaut (who indicates she doesn't care about riding in space, only *working),* would probably frown on the Miss America Pageant and not approve of the new queen, Sharlene Wells (who has no skeletons in her closet), the beauty contest will no doubt continue to pile up more viewers than the NFL.

Maybe "beauty contest" is the wrong choice of words. It is promoted as a "scholarship competition," even though it might suggest that the girls would appear in faded jeans and oversize sweat shirts.

The idea that the girls appear in bathing suits makes some feminists unhappy. Well, looks aren't everything, of course, and money doesn't make people happy, but it is going to be a cold winter on the Amazon before Miss America will be selected by a two-hour written exam.

Beauty contests, or scholarship competitions, or whatever one wants to call them, continue to be popular. Girls enter them from two years old on up. Almost every product in the United States has a little Miss Somebody representing it as a promotional agent. There is an old geezer I know down at the shuffleboard courts who claims he was once a judge for a Miss Plastic Trash Bag and a Miss All Pork Sausage. It's hard to believe.

But there has been a Miss Guernsey Cow Queen, who by no means resembled the product. And everyone is familiar with the Garlic Queen, who no doubt was judged at a distance of not less than 12 feet. She won a certain fame, nonetheless, just as did the Pepperoni Queen and Miss Cement Block.

The only contest winner I ever heard of subject to some misunderstanding was Miss Gum Spirits. She was a beautiful winner in a contest promoted by the turpentine industry, but some of the lesser informed thought it advertised a chewing-gum flavor. A still smaller group thought it was vaguely connected with false teeth.

Despite the aberrations, most of us will continue to want to see products represented by someone beautiful.

FAIR TO MIDDLING

In today's world our lives are being regulated more and more by graphs and statistics.

The statistic that is going the rounds at the present time in the United States and scaring people out of their wits is that the middle class is shrinking.

I cannot believe it. I am sort of middle class myself, and according to the scales in my bathroom I'm not shrinking.

But I know what they mean.

Middle-class people are either getting richer or getting poorer, with the statistical emphasis on the latter. It is not an easy thing to realize one's category is vanishing.

I have a longtime middle-class friend with whom I discuss important things that touch our lives. But when I consulted him on this subject he didn't have much to say.

"Get lost. I'm no longer in your class," he said. "I've joined the poor."

"When did this happen?" I asked, naturally taken aback.

"I'm not sure of the date," he said, "but statistics prove that those who earn between $17,000 and $40,000 a year are middle-class citizens. Last month I found I am averaging only $16,700. Statistically I am with the poor people." A tear came to his eye.

"I'm sorry," I answered. "I suppose we shouldn't have lunch together anymore."

"You're right, of course."

"Things are really tough," I said.

"Well, I haven't given up." He squared his shoulders. "If the middle class can be declared an endangered species, maybe there is hope. Other endangered species are coming back. Look at the whooping crane. And they are saving the whales and eagles. There is even hope for the brown hyena and wild yak. After all, I'm down only $300."

"Sure," I said, "maybe we could even have lunch."

"Well, I suppose at a Burger King."

WOBBLING TENNIS BALLS

It is now fairly well known that in midsummer of this year a baby was born somewhere in the world, probably in Africa, who brought the human population of the earth to more than 5 billion.

Down at the town tennis courts, some of the more expert players have detected a slight wobble in the earth's rotation, causing tennis balls to drift off to the west.

It is amazing, if true, that the mere weight of people on one side of the earth could result in such instability.

As far as my own tennis game is concerned, the alleged wobble has helped somewhat. I always tend to knock balls off to the east. Now they are neutralized.

Perhaps I should leave the town tennis courts out of this, because the surging population is nothing to be sneezed at. Especially since sneezing is not the cause of surplus population.

The debates on the issue are like ecologists speaking out against the vanishing Florida wetlands. They argue awhile, then the wetlands are paved over for a parking lot. It is the argument that is *de rigueur,* not the solution.

It is unlikely that any of the major population issues will be resolved by such debates, but the questions they raise are valid.

A population growing out of control does bring questions of government vs. anarchy on a world scale. It does bring questions of a nation's borders, of national identity and heritage. It does bring questions about the universal workability of Western-style democracy.

Should power, without safeguards or controls, go to people before they are "ready for it"—whatever that means?

It is probably an exaggeration down at the town tennis courts to think the earth is wobbling and that henceforth tennis balls won't fly right.

But it is not hard to imagine that mushrooming population growth could put a strain on many of the world's fragile young democracies.

I think wobbling tennis balls could go on for another 40 years. By that time there will be an additional 3 billion new people.

But who's counting?

BIG BROTHERLY LOVE

1984 has come and gone and George Orwell's Big Brother hasn't arrived.

Maybe Big Brother is just around the corner, like Big Inflation. Ronald Reagan, who was the biggest whatever it was in Washington, could hardly pass himself off as the Orwell-type Big Brother. Except possibly in Grenada.

But in the United States proper (if that is the right term nowadays), he did not have that overawing, omniscient quality that goes with Big Brothership.

Big Granddaddy, maybe.

But who's afraid of the Big Bad Granddaddy? Nobody, unless it is the three little piggybanks holding the savings of Senior Citizens, marginal job holders, and the unemployed.

Big Brotherdom simply has not yet arrived.

The most likely reason America has not been taken over by

BIG BROTHERDOM SIMPLY HAS NOT YET ARRIVED.

Big Brother in 1984 is that George Orwell was wrong.

Unless we can count electrical Big Brothers which have come in the form of Big Computer. Big Computer has a benevolent power, in that it builds automobiles and runs steel mills (at least in Japan).

But they have an ominous side, too, as anyone knows who has become enmeshed in corresponding with one. People have spent a lifetime trying to get their name spelled right or change an incorrect address.

But even with Big Computer, Americans can still spend their day watching television without getting the uneasy feeling that the TV is watching back.

Big Brother may not have come. But the President may unwittingly be setting the stage for the arrival of Big Sister.

THE OTHER LAUGH FEST

A four-day humor conference was held not long ago in Washington.

We don't mean Congress. This was a separate conference at the Shoreham Hotel. Most of the congressmen were away, anyway. Either they were at home on television talking to farmers, or on an important government trip studying soil erosion, at places like the Riviera, the Greek islands, Waikiki Beach, or any warm unfortified area where sand meets with salt water.

Everyone who thought all the comedians have been absorbed into government by now will be relieved to learn there were about 4,000 more-or-less humorous people attending this International Conference on Humor. Also there were an undisclosed number who just came to laugh at the jokes. But they all came from some place other than the nation's capital.

The significance of this meeting is far-reaching. Even if it did not prove to be an earth- or stomach-shaking experience, it does indicate we still have a fund of laugh-getters out there to be tapped for future elections. And, of course, it also indicates there may still be something to laugh at outside of Washington.

That is one of the odd things about Washington. It is the place where something comic is going on all the time, but no one is laughing. Someone once described the Congressional Record as a comic-book horror story. A slight exaggeration, probably.

What do they talk about at a convention of humor? The theme was "What Makes People Laugh?" It was not announced if anything was settled one way or the other as to what makes people laugh, since most of the humor in Washington is unintentional. But no doubt some kind of survey will be made. A government committee is formed to study almost everything.

If a congressional study is made, we would be interested to know why all congressmen are against inflation and deflation but no one comes out in favor of just plain old flation these days.

One last thing. This column is not going to make a federal case out of it, but we weren't invited to the humor convention. Evidently we are not yet funny enough to be in Washington. We intend to keep on trying. But, even more mystifying than our own absence from the convention, there were no senators there either.

GOVERNMENT SECRETS

Spy has become a household word. At the rate spies are being nabbed, one out of every seven Americans must be selling government secrets.

On a recent bus ride I made it a point to study my fellow passengers. I was horrified to discover that practically all of them looked like spies. I suppose you can't tell a spy by his looks. If spies looked like spies they would get caught sooner, instead of running around loose for 20 years.

I decided that the sinister, foreign-looking types around me, with thick eyebrows, were all probably innocent. Either that or various nations hire them to flood the streets as decoys. No, the real spy would turn out to be the sweet, bespectacled, white-haired lady with the enormous knitting bag.

And the spies are all such nice family types. It makes me wonder about organizations such as the PTA and AARP. When a mild-mannered man approached me on the street and asked me where the US Coast Guard station was, I didn't want to tell him. What would a mild-mannered man with rimless glasses, who looked like a vacuum cleaner salesman, want with the location of the Coast Guard? When he explained he owned a power boat

> **I MADE IT A POINT TO STUDY MY FELLOW PASSENGERS. I WAS HORRIFIED TO DISCOVER THAT PRACTICALLY ALL OF THEM LOOKED LIKE SPIES**

and wanted to join the Coast Guard Auxiliary I realized I was being too cautious.

One thing that worried me was a remark made by the President early in December. He emphatically said that the United States "will not hesitate to root out and prosecute the spies of any nation." Any nation? Now that gave me a creepy feeling. It sounded as if hitherto we have been allowing *some* nations to spy on us as a gesture of goodwill. Or maybe the US feels it is in bad taste to nab friendly-nation-type-spies. At any rate, friendly nations seem to have an easier time of it.

Back in the days of Mata Hari nobody fooled around. If a person got caught spying he got shot; after all, he was clearly in the business of shooting *you*. Shooting spies is now considered to be in very bad taste.

Today spying has become more a case for the social worker than the FBI or the Federal Courts. If a person feels he has been mistreated by society this seems to present some justification for selling classified documents to the enemy for large sums of money. Or at least for enough to buy a new car.

APPENDIX

RUN DATE	TITLE	RUN DATE	TITLE
11-22-88	A day of thanks and giving	11-07-84	Grain of hope
10-20-88	A problem of pins and keys	12-29-87	Happy New Year!
07-28-87	A record holder	08-25-88	Is Idaho an Indian name for potato?
03-08-88	A tan at any temperature	09-23-86	It's huge; it's gastronomic
09-14-82	All locked up	12-20-88	Just say Noel
07-14-87	America, the 'henged'	10-24-85	Lessible decibels
08-25-87	Apologies of the abject sort	08-04-82	Living like a sheikh
03-22-88	April is a taxing month	10-02-85	Movie scene
05-15-84	Astro surf	08-12-86	'Mr. Good Guy'
01-19-88	Bean gum syndrome	02-06-89	Musical sleepers
12-19-83	Big brotherly love	05-31-85	News from the bull elephant front
08-21-85	Book of the month		
06-16-88	Bouquets for fathers	12-19-85	Night visitor
10-26-82	Bracken creep	06-27-85	No silence, please
04-14-83	Brother, can you spare a trillion?	02-24-83	North to the what?
02-25-85	Catalog world	04-28-83	Not for the birds
11-08-88	Chandelier munching	06-04-85	Nothing ventured, nothing owed
09-10-87	Charming week		
08-22-83	Chicagophy	03-16-82	Oh, say, can you sing it?
12-03-87	Christmas shopping	05-27-86	One-love for tax reform
11-14-83	Counting others	09-21-82	other laugh fest, The
05-02-85	Cracked records	12-15-87	Pajama talk—on the park bench
07-17-84	D.C. vacation daze		
09-25-84	Fair to middling	11-22-85	Pitching anthems
06-04-82	Finding fault	04-28-88	Post office blues
10-29-87	Fish aren't what they used to be	12-16-85	Rocky roads
03-26-85	Food for thought	05-30-89	Shoeless Guernsey
04-28-82	Forget not the elephant	02-25-86	Soggy kisses
11-26-85	Funny money	04-12-88	sophisticated candy counter, The
05-26-87	Garbage yardage		
02-09-88	Gastronomic ruts	4-11-89	Spring catastrophe
06-02-87	getting of wisdom, The	09-06-88	Squop a wink
06-28-84	Gorgeous exploitation?	10-01-84	There she goes
05-09-84	Government can be taxing	01-12-88	Trivia Day
12-24-85	Government secrets	08-20-85	Trove, anyone?

RUN DATE	TITLE
02-05-86	Tuba city
08-23-88	Watch a whale— and rise on the social scale
08-12-83	What's in a color?
12-08-82	With ketchup
08-26-86	Wobbling tennis balls
03-02-85	Writing on the screen